International
Vegetarian Cuisine

INTERNATIONAL VEGETARIAN CUISINE

by MARIE LOVEJOY

This publication made possible with the
assistance of the Kern Foundation.

The Theosophical Publishing House
Wheaton, Ill. / Madras, India / London, England

Library of Congress Catalog Card No: 77-17691
ISBN: 0-8356-0509-4

Printed in the United States of America

This book is dedicated
to all Man-Kind, as one with all life, for
those who appreciate Nature's gifts to man
and can answer with Appollonius of Tyana:
"We do not wish to add to the troubles of
the animal world."

— Marie Lovejoy

Preface

Whether for moral or health reasons one chooses to follow a vegetarian regime, one must feed the body with a balanced, nutritional diet. There are many books availale that define the contents of foods and inform the vegetarian how to get enough proteins and vitamins. This book is offered for an entirely different reason—that of offering a wide variety of tastes and new or unusual dishes to please the palates of everyone, and to avoid the doldrums of a humdrum diet.

Marie Lovejoy is French-born and has a love of cooking and meal preparation which has been made so evident by these samples of her menus and recipes given here. INTERNATIONAL VEGETARIAN CUISINE presents only a limited selection from her vast collection of gourmet recipes and menus.

Although presented here as complete menus for the most part, you may serve the complete meal or make substitutions from the many other menus for endless variety. Though some recipes may be equally at home in any one of several countries, others are typical.

To tempt your palate, to add new tastes and variety to your meals, to show you that delicious vegetarian dishes are as haute cuisine as any others, we offer you this epicurean trip around the world in your own kitchen.

Editor

Table of Contents

ARABIA (Saudi Arabia)

Saudi Luncheon
Easy Eggplant Patties
Fluffy Steamed Rice
Shish Koftesi in Kofta Bread Pockets
Baked Halves of Tomato
Peach-Ginger Dessert
Coffee

EASY EGGPLANT PATTIES

1	medium size eggplant
20	rich round crackers
1½	cups grated sharp Cheddar cheese
2	minced scallions, white part only
2	slightly beaten eggs
2	tablespoons parsley, freshly snipped
1	clove of garlic, pressed
⅛	teaspoon freshly ground black pepper

Pare the eggplant, cut in cubes, boil covered for 5 minutes. Drain and mash cooked eggplant. Crush the crackers and add the remaining ingredients. Shape the mixture into patties about 3 inches in diameter. In butter or cooking oil (not margarine, as it burns!) sauté patties for about 3 minutes on each side or until golden brown. Serve with fluffy, steamed unpolished rice.

STEAMED UNPOLISHED RICE

Prepare in the usual way.

BAKED TOMATO HALVES
(one or two halves per person)

Carefully cut out the stem part. Cut each tomato in half, crosswise (not from top to bottom). Do not peel. Place halves cut-side up in glass baking dish or pie pan. Sprinkle the top of each with a little salt and pepper — place a half a pat of butter on the top of each half. Cook at 350° F. for 15 minutes. Tomatoes baked this way retain all their juice and are much more delicious than when fried. Baked tomatoes can be reheated afterwards when they are kept in the refrigerator in the same pan in which they were cooked. When wanted, place pan in the oven for a few minutes until warmed through. These are good served for brunch with eggs.

ARAB BREAD (12 buns)

Arab Bread is a round, flat bun with a chewy texture and flavor which resembles that of English Muffins. It can be easily split to make a pocket to hold a ground vegetarian "meat" patty and chopped vegetables. Traditionally it is used to make a sandwich which Arabians call "Kofta."

1 package yeast, active dry or compressed
2 cups warm water (lukewarm for compressed yeast)
1 teaspoon salt
4½ cups unsifted flour

Pour the water into a large bowl; add the yeast and stir until dissolved. Add the salt and gradually stir in the flour, beating until smooth dough forms. Scrape dough down from sides of bowl, cover lightly, and let rise in a warm place until doubled (about 1 hour). Stir down; divide into 12 parts, placing them on a well-floured board. Cover lightly and let stand for 30 minutes. Place two of the dough mounds on a lightly greased and floured cooky sheet. With fingers, press lightly around the edge of the dough to flatten and shape into rounds about 5 inches in diameter and ½ inch thick. (Try not to squeeze out air bubbles; instead, force them to the center of the bread.)

With oven shelf at lowest possible level, bake in a moderate oven (350° F.) for about 20 minutes. (The bun should puff up but will not be brown.)

When all the buns are baked, place under a broiler for about 1 minute to brown the tops lightly. Let cool. Use immediately, or wrap in plastic film, or plastic bags to store. This bread freezes well, or will keep in the refrigerator about 1 week. To serve "Shish Koftesi": Split open the bun about ⅓ of the way around; open it up to make a pocket. Butter the inside of the bun pocket, then slip in a hot burger patty and serve with your choice of relishes.

SHISH KOFTESI (Vegetarian Burger)

1 can (20 oz.) vegetarian burger
1 can (Size 2½) tomatoes, drained
1 green pepper, minced
1 cup minced onion
1 clove garlic, pureed
4 beaten eggs
¼ pound butter (1 stick)
½ teaspoon freshly ground black pepper
  Salt to taste

Sauté the onion and green pepper in butter until onion is golden. Add canned burger material and drained tomatoes. Cover and simmer over low heat until the mixture is steamed through. While the mixture is still hot, pour over it the beaten eggs and stir gently until the eggs are cooked. Add seasonings. (If you do not like a soupy mixture, omit or reduce the amount of tomatoes.)

ARABIAN "KOFTA SANDWICH"

Have ready a mixture of fresh vegetables, about equal portions each of chopped lettuce, green pepper, green onions, and celery. Butter the inside pocket of Arab bread; put in 2 or 3 tablespoons of the vegetable mixture; slip in 1 hot Shish Koftesi burger patty; add more chopped fresh vegetables on the top. Serve immediately.

PEACH-GINGER DESSERT

1 3-oz. package orange or peach gelatin
1 cup ginger ale
    Water
¼ cup finely chopped pecans
¾ cup chopped fresh peaches
½ cup thinly sliced crystalized ginger
    Whipped cream
½ teaspoon almond extract

Use 3 oz. of orange or peach gelatin (vegetarian gelatin or any non-animal tissue brand sold in health food stores or where Kosher products are available.) Substitute 1 cup ginger ale for 1 cup of the water in the recipe. Remember that agar-agar gelatin jells more quickly than gelatin made from animal tissues. As soon as the mixture begins to thicken slightly, add ¼ cup of finely chopped pecans and ¾ cup chopped fresh peaches. (Frozen or canned may be substituted.) Fold in ½ cup of thinly sliced crystallized or candied ginger. Chill in 5-oz. stemmed sherbet compotes. If you cannot get the orange or peach flavored gelatin, use orange juice as part of required liquid, but do not change the proportions of liquid. This dessert may be topped with a little sweetened whipped cream, with ½ teaspoon almond extract added after whipping.

ARGENTINA

An Argentine Buffet
Avocado Dip with Corn Chips
Ensalada Russa — Ensalada de Pocho
Meatless Chicken Rings with
Stuffed Eggs — Roasted Sweet Peppers — Mixed Olives
Hot Buttered Garlic Bread
Pastel de Choclo (Argentine Corn Pie)
Ice Tea   Coffee

AVOCADO DIP

For a tempting appetizer served with corn chips, this is an excellent dip.

2 large ripe avocados
3 tablespoons lime juice
½ cup minced scallions (white part only)
1 can (4 oz.) green chiles
1 diced ripe tomato

Dice the tomato and scallions. Peel and remove pit from two ripe avocados and mash them. Immediately sprinkle them with the lime juice to prevent their turning brown. Add to the mashed avocados a small can, drained, of green chiles, the scallions and diced tomatoes. Serve in a small bowl surrounded by crisp corn chips for dipping. Corn chips are best for this dip.

ENSALADA RUSSA

4 large potatoes, cooked and peeled
3 or 4 medium carrots, peeled
1 package (9 oz.) frozen cut green beans
1 can diced beets (about 8 oz.)

¾ cup olive oil or salad oil
   Romaine lettuce leaves
½ cup wine vinegar
1 teaspoon salt
¼ teaspoon pepper
½ cup mayonnaise
   Chopped parsley

Dice the cooked potatoes and place in a large bowl. Steam the carrots in a small amount of salted water until tender crisp. Cook frozen green beans in the same pan of salted water, boiling for 8 to 10 minutes, then drain and add to the potatoes. Slice the carrots and add them to the potatoes and green beans. Drain the beets and rinse with water 2 or 3 times, then set aside. Combine the oil, vinegar, salt and pepper in a jar; shake to mix and pour over the bowl of diced vegetables. Refrigerate for at least 2 hours, stirring once or twice. Shortly before serving, add the beets to the mixture, then drain off the marinade (oil and vinegar mixture). Carefully mix the mayonnaise with the vegetables and turn into a serving bowl lined with Romaine lettuce leaves; ruby lettuce sets this dish off very well, too. Sprinkle chopped parsley over the top and serve. (Mayonnaise recipe given in France section.) Serves 8.

ENSALADA DE POCHO

1 head Romaine lettuce
1 head butter lettuce (or Bibb)
3 tomatoes, medium size, peeled and cut into eighths

DRESSING

½ cup salad oil, preferably part olive oil
¼ cup vinegar
1 whole clove garlic, peeled
2 tablespoons chopped celery
2 to 3 teaspoons of capers
½ teaspoon of salt
½ teaspoon oregano
⅛ teaspoon dry mustard
⅛ teaspoon pepper

Make the dressing a day or two in advance by combining the ingredients in a jar with tight lid and refrigerate until ready to use. Remove the garlic clove before serving.

Wash, drain and chill the two varieties of lettuce. Tear these greens in small pieces and add tomatoes, dressing and toss. Serve immediately.

ICE TEA (Thé Glacé)

Pre-sweeten the tea and serve in tall, chilled glasses with a slice of lemon, a sprig of mint and a cherry in each glass.

MEATLESS CHICKEN RINGS

Vegetarian chicken substitute comes in several forms and is sold under various brand names. If you use the canned type, chill first; if you prepare this dish with the frozen variety, which comes already sliced in rounds, defrost first. Arrange round slices on a large platter or serving tray. (To serve 8 you will need 2 packages, 13 oz. each.) Around the outside of the platter arrange artistically stuffed hardcooked eggs, both ripe and green olives, and large chunks of roasted red and green pepper.

PASTEL DE CHOCLO
(Argentine Corn Pie)

2 packages frozen white or yellow corn (10 oz. each)
4 eggs, beaten lightly
¾ cup milk
1 cup sugar
2½ cups soft bread crumbs
½ teaspoon vanilla
Dash of salt

Thaw 2 packages of frozen cut corn. Mash it or whirl it in a blender until nearly smooth. Lightly beat 4 eggs in a large bowl. Mix in the corn; add milk, sugar and soft bread crumbs. Add vanilla and dash of salt. Spoon this mixture into a well-greased 9" x 13" baking pan. Bake in a moderate oven (375°F.) for about 50 minutes or until nicely browned. Cool, cover and chill in refrigerator for at least 3 hours (or as long as 3 days). To serve, cut in squares and top with sweetened whipped cream.

AUSTRALIA

Tomato Soup
Mixed Green Salad
Vegetable Nut Roast with Brown Gravy
Creamed Spinach
Cantaloupe Halves filled with Vanilla Ice Cream
Beverage

TOMATO SOUP WITH VARIATIONS

You can vary prepared canned tomato soup by adding a small amount of sautéed chopped onion, celery, and a little bouillon or stock made from a vegetarian cube, but this is not necessary.

MIXED GREEN SALAD

A combination can be made of any of the following greens: Romaine lettuce, escarole, endive, chicory, Boston lettuce, Simpson lettuce, watercress, bibb (Kentucky limestone) lettuce. Wash carefully and replace in cellophane bag in refrigerator to get crisp. When ready to serve, wipe dry in paper toweling, or shake in a French wire basket. Tear the leaves (do not cut them). Add French dressing or cold pressed olive oil and lemon juice. Serve powdered kelp instead of salt for dieters. (Tomatoes are not served with this classic salad.)

VEGETABLE NUT ROAST

1 cup walnut meats
3 onions, chopped fine
1 cup celery, diced fine
1 green pepper, seeded and chopped (optional)
5 carrots
4 slices bread
1 or 2 eggs
½ teaspoon ground thyme
Salad oil for cooking

Sauté chopped onions, celery, and green pepper in 4 tablespoons oil for about 5 minutes. Put through a food chopper the carrots, nuts, and bread torn in small pieces. Add to sautéed mixture with thyme and slightly beaten eggs. Add salt and pepper to taste. Pour into a well-buttered bread pan and top with cracker crumbs dotted with butter. Bake in a 350° F. oven for about 40 minutes or until brown. Serve with the sauce given below. Serves 6.

cool mixture by placing pan in a larger pan of cold water to hasten cooling process. When mixture is cool, beat the egg whites until stiff (an electric beater is handy for so many egg whites). They should stand up in a point when the egg beater is lifted out. Do not overbeat egg whites. If they are too stiff, you will have to work hard to incorporate them into the base and thus break too many of the balloon bubbles, lose too much of the air, hence the lifting power of the whites will be curtailed. Gently fold the beaten whites into the cooled cheese mixture. With spoon cut down through the egg white to the bottom of the big bowl, then bring the spoon along the bottom of the bowl and up over egg white, cutting down again through it. Continue to cut and fold until egg white disappears.

Pour the batter into a well-buttered 12-cup straight-sided soufflé dish which should be ¾ to ⅞ full. Do not use any other kind of dish. Set dish in a big pan of water in a moderate oven (375° F.). Bake for 15 minutes, then slightly increase the heat to 400° F. for another 18 minutes. Do not open oven door to look at soufflé from the time you put it in the oven. Make certain to have preheated the oven before starting to cook. Three to four more minutes may be added, for this amount is double the regular recipe. The soufflé will rise high and be a rich brown color when baked. Do not plan to cook other foods in the same oven at the same time. Serve immediately.

If you have a second oven, use it to heat sturdy French bread, to be served with unsalted butter.

CARROTS AUSTRALIAN

5 large, tender carrots
2 tablespoons butter
2 tablespoons lemon juice
1 teaspoon sugar
  Salt
  Chopped, fresh parsley

Scrub and dice 5 large, tender carrots and cook in a small amount of water which barely covers them. Drain immediately so that they do not become waterlogged. Reheat with two tablespoons of butter, two tablespoons lemon juice, a little salt, one teaspoon of sugar and a little chopped, fresh parsley. Serves two.

FRESH PEACH TAPIOCA

2 cups sliced fresh peaches
2 tablespoons butter
1 cup granulated sugar
⅓ cup quick-cooking tapioca
2 tablespoons brown sugar
2½ cups water
½ teaspoon salt
¼ teaspoon nutmeg
¼ teaspoon grated lemon rind
1 tablespoon lemon juice
1 teaspoon almond extract

Combine peaches, butter, sugar, tapioca, brown sugar, salt, nutmeg, lemon rind, water and lemon juice, in a saucepan. Let stand 5 minutes. Cook and stir over medium heat until mixture comes to a boil. Reduce heat and simmer 2 minutes or until peaches are tender. Remove from heat. Add almond extract. Pour into serving bowls or glass dishes. Serve warm, with whipped cream if desired. Makes 4½ cups or 8 servings.

Australian Summer Lunch

Australian Summer Borscht Made Easy
Swiss Cheese Soufflé
Australian Carrots
Hot Parker House Rolls
Fresh Peach Tapioca
Beverage

AUSTRALIAN SUMMER BORSCHT MADE EASY (1½ quarts)

1 quart jar commercially canned clear Borscht
1 pint dairy sour cream
  Freshly snipped dill (or dried dillweed — not dill seed)
  Cucumber slices or sticks

In electric blender combine 2 cups borscht and 1 cup sour cream. Blend, covered, at high speed for about 20 seconds. Pour into serving pitcher or bowl. Blend the remaining borscht and sour cream and refrigerate, covered, until serving time. To serve, pour into chilled serving bowls, garnish with a sprinkling of fresh dill. Float a thin slice of cucumber on the surface. This may also be served in short, wide-mouth glasses, in which you use cucumber stick "stirrers" rather than a slice on top. Serves 8.

SWISS CHEESE SOUFFLÉ

4 tablespoons butter
4 tablespoons flour
1½ cups milk, heated
8 oz. (½ pound) Gruyère (Swiss) cheese
8 egg yolks
12 egg whites
1¼ teaspoons dry mustard
3 teaspoons sugar
¼ teaspoon cayenne pepper
1 teaspoon salt

Mix last 4 items in 4 teaspoons water. Melt butter in skillet over low flame. Then, keeping pan over slow flame, mix in flour thoroughly. Add Swiss cheese grated, and keep slowly stirring until it partially melts and looks curdled. Add gradually the warm milk, stirring the mixture constantly. Continue stirring until the cheese is all melted and no lumps can be seen. Add seasonings already mixed together. Beat egg yolks until thick and lemon-colored. Add them to the cheese mixture (still over a very slow fire) and stir until the mixture is like a very thick custard. Remove skillet from stove and

18

BROWN GRAVY
for Vegetable Nut Roast

3 tablespoons butter
3 tablespoons flour
   A few drops of onion juice
   Salt and pepper
½ pound mushrooms, fresh or canned, sliced
1 tablespoon vegetable protein
1½ cups milk

Melt butter and add flour as in preparing to make white sauce. Stir until flour is slightly golden; add milk gradually. Stir constantly until starch is thoroughly cooked. Add sliced mushrooms which have been previously sautéed in butter; add onion juice, salt and pepper, and soy protein.

Select firm, ripe cataloupe by pressing end with thumb; it should give slightly but not be too soft. You should always smell the melon and thereby see if the aroma is full. See Index for French Vanilla Ice Cream.

CREAMED SPINACH

Allow 2 pounds of spinach for 4 people. Wash thoroughly in several cold waters. Remove all tough stems, chop finely. Put in large kettle and barely cover with boiling water. Place lid on kettle and cook no longer than 2 to 5 minutes. Drain well in colander, using the back of a wooden spoon to squeeze water out of spinach. Add a pinch of nutmeg to a white sauce made with 2 tablespoons melted butter in a saucepan with 2 tablespoons flour and 1 cup milk. Stir until thickened and well cooked. Add salt and pepper. Mix sauce with chopped hot spinach which can be reheated by stirring over low heat.

AUSTRIA (Vienna)

A Viennese Dinner
Viennese Fresh Asparagus Soup
Watercress and Grape Salad
Cream Cheese in Ramekins
Cucumbers Viennese
Buttered Beets
Hot Rolls with Sweet, Unsalted Butter
Vanilla Poppy Seed Cake
Demi tasse

VIENNESE FRESH ASPARAGUS SOUP

1 or 2 bunches fresh asparagus (depending on number of servings)
3 Salted water
3 tablespoons butter
3 tablespoons flour
   Dash of pepper
   Unsweetened whipped cream

Clean asparagus and cut off tips, putting them to one side. In salted water, place the stalk ends, cut into small pieces and discarding the tough, stringy ones and boil until tender. When these stalk pieces are soft, put them in a blender or through a sieve. In a separate saucepan melt the 3 tablespoons of butter and stir in flour over low heat until butter is golden, but not brown. Add this to the asparagus water and pulp and add in the tender tips, stirring together; allow mixture to come to a boil. Boil gently for about 10 minutes, or until the tips are tender. Be careful not to overcook or the tips will break apart. Add a dash of pepper, but not too much as asparagus has a delicate flavor. Ladle carefully into cups or soup plates and just before serving, add a tablespoon of unsweetened whipped cream to top off each dish. Serve with croutons. (See Index.)

WATERCRESS AND GRAPE SALAD

1 bundle of watercress (fresh and crisp)
8 oz. pecan nutmeats (1 lb. serves 8)
   French dressing
1 orange
1 cup grapes (either white seedless or halve and seed pink grapes)

Wash watercress carefully and drain. Arrange with thin slices of orange and grapes and the nut meats. Do not serve with any dressing any stronger flavored than French dressing. You can use Chantilly dressing if you prefer (see Philippines menu).

Serve hot rolls or warm crusty Vienna Twist bread and butter with this luncheon.

CREAM CHEESE IN RAMEKINS

2 packages cream cheese (3 oz. each)
¼ cup milk
4 eggs, beaten
½ teaspoon salt
1 teaspoon dry mustard

Heat the cream cheese in top of double boiler until soft. Add remaining ingredients and blend thoroughly. Pour mixture into ramekins or individual custard cups and place in pan of water (1 inch deep). Bake in oven heated to 325°F. for 20 to 25 minutes. Serves 4.

CUCUMBERS VIENNESE

2 medium size firm cucumbers
2 teaspoons finely minced parsley
3 teaspoons sour cream
   Pinch of salt
   Lemon juice
   Salad oil

Peel cucumbers and slice very thin. Add a pinch of salt, mix well and put in refrigerator for about an hour. Make a dressing of 1 part lemon juice to 3 parts of oil and add 2 teaspoons very finely minced parsley. Add 3 teaspoons of sour cream and beat together with fork and pour over the cucumbers. Serve in a shallow, and not too large, serving dish.

BUTTERED BEETS

Use tiny round beets or the julienne (shoestring) in the small cans. It will take 2 cans for 4 servings. Heat, drain and season with melted butter on top. Be sure to drain well so that beet juice will not run over the plate onto other foods.

VANILLA SUGAR

Vanilla sugar flavors a cake! Nothing is more easily made than vanilla sugar. Split a vanilla bean down the center, cut into 1-inch pieces, and tuck these pieces into two pounds of sifted confectioner's powdered sugar which is tightly covered in a jar. After a period of at least two weeks, you will find this sugar to be permeated with the most heavenly fragrance of vanilla, ready for all kinds of wonderful baking and preparation of desserts.

VANILLA POPPY SEED CAKE

2 cups all-purpose flour
1 cup poppy seeds
2 teaspoons baking powder
⅛ teaspoon salt
½ cup real butter
1½ cups vanilla sugar (see above)
4 eggs
¾ cup milk

Combine flour, poppy seeds, baking powder and salt and set aside. In a large electric mixer bowl, blend butter and sugar until light and fluffy. Beat in the eggs, one at a time, beating well after each addition. Set mixer at low speed and beat in half of the flour mixture; blend one minute. Add milk and blend one more minute. Add remaining flour mixture and blend another minute.

Grease well and lightly flour a 9-inch tube cake pan; pour in cake batter. Pre-heat oven to 350° F. and bake 55 minutes, or until a cake tester inserted near the center comes out clean. Allow to cool in inverted pan 10 minutes before removing to a wire rack to finish cooling. Frost with creamy vanilla frosting.

CREAMY VANILLA FROSTING

¼ cup real butter, softened
¼ cup light cream or milk
3 cups vanilla confectioner's sugar

Beat butter until fluffy and add confectioner's sugar alternately with cream until well blended and smooth. Makes 1⅔ cups frosting. With a wide spatula, spread frosting over top and sides of the 9-inch tube cake.

NOTE: In place of vanilla sugar, use one teaspoon pure vanilla extract (no substitute) for each cup of sugar. Add to batter and beat.

BAHAMA ISLANDS

Corn Chowder Lunch
Easy Corn Chowder
Vinaigrette Vegetable Mold
Orange Pecan Muffins
Sunshine Cake with Orange Sauce
Tea

EASY CORN CHOWDER

4 small white onions, chopped fine
2 tablespoons butter
1 cup grated carrots
1 can (#2 size) whole kernel corn
1 can cream of mushroom soup
1 cup milk
1 cup light cream
½ teaspoon salt
¼ teaspoon white pepper
 Chopped fresh parsley

Skin 4 small white onions, slice finely, and chop. Brown slightly in 2 tablespoons butter with 1 cup grated carrots. Cook together until tender. Watch carefully so as not to char while cooking. Mix 1 can (#2) whole kernel yellow corn, 1 can cream of mushroom soup, 1 cup milk, 1 cup light cream, ½ teaspoon salt and ¼ teaspoon white pepper. Heat thoroughly (but do not boil). Add contents of skillet, scraping all the butter and all the vegetables in each serving. Sprinkle each cup with chopped parsley. Serves 4.

VINAIGRETTE VEGETABLE MOLD

1 tablespoon agar-agar (seaweed) vegetarian unflavored or lemon gelatin, (follow directions on pkg.)
¼ cup water (follow directions on pkg. of unflavored or lemon gelatin.
1 can (16 oz.) cut asparagus or green beans, or part of both
1 jar (6 oz.) marinated artichoke hearts, drained
½ cup sliced stuffed green olives
1 tablespoon minced green onion
⅓ cup sugar
1 teaspoon salt
⅓ cup white wine vinegar
½ cup finely diced seeded green pepper

Soften gelatin as indicated on package. Add water to juice from asparagus or beans to make one cup (or use water alone). Bring to a boil and stir in gelatin until dissolved. Cool until almost set and fold in remaining ingredients. Be watchful, as vegetarian gelatin sets much quicker than the rennet kind. Turn into 1 quart mold and chill until firm. Serve on lettuce leaves, with mayonnaise, garnished with stuffed hard cooked eggs.

ORANGE PECAN MUFFINS

1¾ cups flour, all-purpose
2 eggs, separated
¼ cup milk
3 teaspoons baking powder
¼ teaspoon salt
¼ cup orange juice
⅓ cup butter
¾ cup sugar
1 tablespoon orange rind
¾ cup chopped pecans

Cream shortening, add sugar. Separate eggs and add yolks to sugar mixture and beat well. To the milk, add juice and grated rind. Then sift flour with baking powder and salt and add to milk mixture alternating with the eggs. Add chopped pecans. Fold in the stiffly beaten egg whites. Fill greased 3-inch muffin pans ⅔ full and bake in oven pre-heated to 375° F. for 20 to 25 minutes, or until golden brown.

SUNSHINE CAKE

6 egg yolks
1 teaspoon lemon extract and
1 teaspoon orange extract mixed
1 cup granulated sugar
2 teaspoons baking powder
½ cup hot water
  Grated rind of 1 orange
  Grated rind of ½ lemon
1½ cups cake flour, sifted before measuring
1½ teaspoons salt

For this delicious, light, golden sponge cake, the most important step is the thorough beating of the egg yolks—before and after adding the sugar! With a rotary beater, beat the six egg yolks until thick and lemon color. Gradually add the sugar and the flavorings and continue the beating. Sift all dry ingredients together and add to egg mixture alternately with the hot water. Beat well after each addition. Pour batter into an ungreased angel cake pan or a 9-inch tube pan; bake for 1 hour in a slow oven (350°F.) or 45 minutes if oven is heated to 375°F. Oven settings for recipes always mean to have oven pre-heated to the specified temperature unless otherwise instructed. After baking, invert the pan and let the cake cool with air circulating beneath it. If you do not have a wire rack for this purpose, you can prop the pan up on cups, or spring clothespins can be attached to the rim to serve as legs to support it in an inverted position. Serve the cake plain, or with the following Orange Sauce.

ORANGE SAUCE

1½ cups granulated sugar
½ cup flour
½ cup cold water
1½ cups boiling water
  Grated rind of 1 orange
  Pinch of salt, very small
  Juice of 2 oranges and 1 lemon
3 eggs separated

Mix flour, sugar, grated orange rind, salt, and place in top of a double boiler. Add cold water and stir until smooth, then pour in the boiling water stirring constantly until smoothly thickened. Let cook over hot water for 10 to 15 minutes. Add fruit juices and stir in the well-beaten egg yolks. Again stir constantly for 2 or 3 minutes longer.

When cake is cool, break it into a shallow glass- or earthenware baking dish and pour the hot sauce over it. Cover with a meringue made of the stiffly beaten and sweetened egg whites.

Brown the meringue topping lightly in a slow oven of 325°. Serve the pudding either warm or cold. A sprinkling of coconut may be added before the meringue for a variety. For an extra fancy touch, the meringue may be garnished with orange sections, free of any membrane, and rolled in granulated sugar.

TEA
Peel part of a fresh ginger root and cut a thin slice to drop in each boiling hot cup of tea — this gives it a wonderful flavor!

BELGIUM

A Belgian Dinner

Walnut Rice Loaf
Brussel Sprouts with Chestnuts
or
Broccoli and Artichoke Hearts
Chicory Salad à la Provence
Hard Rolls
Apricot Soufflé with Fruit Sauce
or
Fruits in Season with Brie Cheese
Coffee

BELGIAN WALNUT RICE LOAF

1 cup ground walnuts
2 cups rice, cooked half done
1 large stalk of celery
6 onions, chopped
2 cloves pressed garlic
1 green pepper, chopped
½ bunch parsley, chopped
  Butter
1 can (20 oz.) tomatoes
1 egg
½ pound grated sharp cheddar cheese or
  other cheese of your choice
1 teaspoon ground thyme
3 bay leaves
  Salt and pepper to taste
1 cup Safflower oil

Sauté chopped vegetables in the oil. When soft, but not brown, add the tomatoes with its juice, the bay leaves, garlic, salt, pepper and thyme. Simmer gently for 5 minutes. Then add the partly cooked rice, the nuts, and minced parsley. Blend all together then add the beaten egg. Place the mixture in a well-oiled bread pan or baking dish and sprinkle with the grated cheese and dot with butter. Bake in a 350° F. oven for 45 minutes. To serve you may sprinkle the top with chopped olives, if you wish, or serve with a hot tomato sauce to vary it. In Europe this is frequently prepared a day ahead, up to the point of adding the beaten egg, and added before baking. The loaf can also be served with mayonnaise when cold. It is also served on a bed of lettuce as a cold buffet dish with salad and hot rolls.

BRUSSELS SPROUTS WITH CHESTNUTS

1 to 1½ lbs. fresh, or 2 pkgs. frozen Brussels
  Sprouts
1 pound chestnuts

¼ cup butter
2 teaspoons sugar
Salt

Remove the shells from 1 pound of chestnuts. Cut 2 gashes in the form of a cross on the flat side of each nut with a pointed knife. Blanch by placing nuts in oven at 400°F. for 15 minutes, or boil them in water for the same length of time, then drain. When nuts are cool enough to handle, break off the outer shell.

Wash Brussel Sprouts carefully, removing outer discolored leaves and cutting off the stems. Cook in boiling salted water until tender. Drain. Put ¼ cup of butter with 2 teaspoons sugar in pan, stirring constantly, cook until brown, then add chestnuts and brown them. Mix the nuts and browned butter into the Brussel Sprouts. Season further if you wish. Green beans can also be served in this same way.

BROCCOLI AND ARTICHOKE HEARTS WITH MORNAY SAUCE

1 bunch broccoli
  Salt
1 jar artichoke hearts
  Swiss Cheese, grated
  Paprika

Cook the broccoli in salted water until tender having removed tough portions of stalk. Make sure the broccoli is well covered with the boiling water the entire time or it will turn brown. Drain and place in a buttered baking dish, with 1 jar of artichoke hearts. Pour Mornay sauce over them and sprinkle with grated cheese and dashes of paprika, and bake in an oven heated to 350°F. until crusty.

**Chicory Salad à la Provence
(see Italy menus for recipe)**

MORNAY SAUCE

2 tablespoons butter
1 cup milk
½ Swiss Cheese, grated
2 egg yolks, slightly beaten
2 tablespoons flour
  Salt and paprika

Melt butter, blend in flour and add milk gradually to make a white sauce. Gradually add grated Swiss cheese, then salt and paprika to taste. Stir in the beaten egg yolks and continue stirring until smooth. Pour over the vegetable mix and top with more grated cheese and dashes of paprika.

APRICOT SOUFFLÉ WITH FRUIT SAUCE

1 cup apricot pulp, mashed or blended
4 eggs, separated (need 2 at a time only)
  juice and grated rind of 1 orange
⅓ cup sugar
  Whipped cream, optional

Heat one cup of apricot pulp (pressed through a sieve or put in a blender), sweeten to taste. Beat egg whites until stiff and gradually mix into apricot pulp, then pour into a buttered and sugared casserole dish. Bake for 40 minutes at 350° F.

Separate two more egg whites and beat until stiff. Beat the yolks and add the juice and grated rind of 1 orange, and ⅓ cup of sugar. Cook the egg yolk mixture in a double boiler until thick; cool and add to the stiffly beaten egg whites. Pour over Apricot Soufflé. Top with whipped cream if you like.

BRAZIL

Brazilian Sunday Dinner
Vegetarian Nut Croquettes
Baked Cucumber Cheese Boats
Baked Tomatoes
Brazilian Rice
Cold Steamed Asparagus with Sauce Vinaigrette
Hot chunks of French Bread with Garlic Butter
Brazilian Chocolate
Juicy, spicy Red-Gold Cranshaw Melon
with Lime Wedges

VEGETARIAN NUT CROQUETTES

1 cup walnuts or any good meat substitute (20 oz.)
¼ cup stuffed green olives, chopped
½ cup celery, chopped fine
½ cup onion, chopped fine
4 eggs, beaten
¾ cup fine bread crumbs
2 tablespoons parsley, minced fine
½ clove garlic, peeled and crushed
½ teaspoon salt
¼ teaspoon pepper
Peanut oil for frying

Grind walnuts fine (or mash meat substitute), add celery, onion, olives, parsley, garlic and seasonings. Mix all with beaten eggs, shape into croquettes, and fry. If you wish you can dip the uncooked croquettes before pan or deep frying in beaten egg and cracker crumbs. Serve immediately. Makes 10.

BAKED TOMATOES

1 tomato per serving, select ripe but firm ones
Salt
Pepper
Butter
Dash of dill weed, if you like

Carefully cut out the stem mark. You will serve each person two halves or use half red and half yellow tomatoes serving one half of each color to guests. Cut tomatoes around the middle, not from top to bottom. Do not peel. Place halves, cut side up, in a shallow baking dish or pan. Sprinkle tops with salt and pepper, and add a dab of butter to the top of each. Heat oven to 350°F. and bake tomatoes for 15 minutes. This is long enough to heat through, but they will retain their juices and are much more flavorful than fried tomatoes. They may be reheated, if they are left in baking dish and kept covered in refrigerator. They will be as tasty reheated as they were when first prepared.

Baked tomatoes are delicious served as an accompaniment with eggs, even for breakfast. They can be prepared in greater quantity than needed for a meal since they can be refrigerated and reheated.

BAKED CUCUMBER CHEESE BOATS

1 cup (½ pound) butter
½ cup white flour
¼ teaspoon cayenne pepper (not more)
2 teaspoons salt
6 cups milk
1½ cups sharp cheddar cheese grated and firmly packed
3 cups Swiss cheese, grated and firmly packed
6 small cucumbers
4 cups cooked unpolished rice
2 tablespoons Worcestershire sauce or soy sauce
¼ cup lemon juice
1 teaspoon salt
2 packages (2½ oz. each) toasted slivered almonds

Prepare rice and set aside.

In double boiler, melt one half of the butter. Blend flour, butter, salt and pepper. Add milk gradually, stirring constantly, and cook until mixture thickens. Add cheddar and Swiss cheese, stirring occasionally until cheese is melted.

Peel cucumbers thinly and cut in half lengthwise. Carefully scrape out the seeds and sauté cucumber halves in remainder of butter for 2 minutes on each side. Place hollowed side up in a shallow baking dish. Fill cucum-bers with cooked rice. Add Worcestershire (or soy) sauce, lemon juice, and 1 teaspoon salt to remaining butter and sprinkle over cucumbers Mask each cucumber boat with cheese sauce. Scatter slivered almonds on top of each boat. Bake at 350°F. for 35 minutes. Serve immediately. Serves 6.

COLD STEAMED ASPARAGUS

2 bunches of fresh green asparagus
Salt
Water

Clean and cut off the lower, tough stems. Loosely tie the asparagus so that it will stand upright in the deep sauce pan. Add salt to just enough water to steam asparagus. If you are using a mesh steamer insert in the pan, do not let the water quite reach the steamer. Steam until tender but be careful not to overcook. Drain and chill in refrigerator until time to serve.

SAUCE VINAIGRETTE (Serves 8)

1 teaspoon salt
1 teaspoon paprika
¼ teaspoon pepper
6 tablespoon vinegar
1 tablespoon parsley, finely chopped
8 tablespoons olive oil
1 tablespoon olives or pickles, finely chopped
1 tablespoon green pepper, finely chopped

Place all ingredients in a small Mason jar with rubber ring. Screw lid on tight and shake well, or place in a bowl and beat with a rotary egg beater. When thoroughly combined, the mixture will become thick. Mix in the chopped olives or pickles, the pepper and parsley. This sauce is excellent served on cold asparagus, too.

BRAZILIAN RICE

- 2 small onions, chopped
- 2 cloves garlic, crushed
- 2 tablespoons vegetable oil
- 4 medium tomatoes, peeled and chopped
- 1 bay leaf
- 2 cups long-grain rice, uncooked
- ⅛ teaspoon pepper

Sauté 2 small chopped onions and 2 crushed cloves of garlic in 2 tablespoons of vegetable oil until tender, but not brown. Add 4 medium tomatoes (peeled and chopped), 1 bay leaf, 2 cups uncooked long grain rice, 1 teaspoon salt in 4½ cups of water and ⅛ teaspoon pepper. Cook this mixture until the rice absorbs the liquid. Then stir in 3 cups of boiling water, cover and continue cooking until the rice is just tender. Makes 12 servings.

BRAZILIAN CHOCOLATE
("Chocolat Brasilien")

- ½ cup cocoa (not instant)
- ¼ cup sugar
- 1 cup water
- 3 cups milk
- 1 tablespoon grated orange rind
- ¼ teaspoon almond extract
   Cinnamon sticks

Blend the cocoa with the sugar, gradually stir in the water and the milk. Heat to the boiling point. Add the orange rind and almond extract. Chill. Before serving, beat with a rotary beater until frothy. Serve with a cinnamon stick in each cup. Makes 1 quart. This chocolate is usually served at tea time or late at night after theatre hours. It can also double as a dessert.

BULGARIA

A Bulgarian Menu

Buttermilk Soup
"Fassouliahnia" — Bulgarian White Beans in Olive Oil
Steamed Beet Tops
Vegetable Macedoine Salad
Poached Ginger Pears
Tea

BUTTERMILK SOUP

3 egg yolks
½ cup sugar
4 cups buttermilk (1 quart)
1 teaspoon lemon juice
1 teaspoon vanilla
½ teaspoon grated lemon rind
½ cup cream, whipped

Beat the egg yolks with an electric mixer and gradually add the sugar. When it forms a ribbon, add the lemon juice and grated lemon rind, then the vanilla. Very slowly, beat in the buttermilk until smooth. Serve in your best bowls which have been chilled, and garnish with slivers of blanched almonds, whipped cream or whole raspberries, or even sprinkled with chopped fresh mint leaves.

FASSOULIAHNIA —
Bulgarian White Beans in Olive Oil

2 cans (20 oz. each) white kidney beans, drained

½ cup minced parsley
1 green pepper, seeded and diced
¼ cup onion, chopped
2 cloves garlic, peeled and pressed
2 teaspoons sugar
½ teaspoon salt
¼ cup olive oil
3 tablespoons lemon juice
⅛ teaspoon white pepper

In a large bowl combine drained beans with parsley, green pepper, onion and garlic. In a cup, mix the sugar, salt, pepper, olive oil and lemon juice. Dribble this mixture over the beans. Toss lightly to mix and marinate for at least an hour to let seasonings completely permeate the dish. After marinated and heated, add 2 thinly sliced raw tomatoes to the garnish. This salad is served hot.

STEAMED LEAVES OF NEW BEETS

Select only the freshest tender leaves of new beets. Prepare the same as you would spinach, washing well, draining, and cutting out the large center stems. Steam until just tender and chop fine. Add butter and garnish with sliced tomatoes. This is either a vegetable or a salad dish, but it is generally served hot. Beet greens are an alkaline food and help to counteract acids in the blood stream. Beet tops should be eaten frequently by persons suffering with high blood pressure.

VEGETABLE MACEDOINE SALAD

1   9-oz. pkg. frozen green beans, cooked
1   10-oz. pkg. frozen lima beans, cooked
1   10-oz. pkg. frozen cauliflower, cooked
4   boiled, diced, potatoes
1   clove garlic, minced
    Minced scallions or chives
1   9-oz. pkg. frozen asparagus tips, cooked
    Lettuce
2   beets, steamed, peeled and chopped
    Raw carrot sticks or diced carrot
1   10-oz. pkg. frozen green peas, cooked
    Celery, sliced in shoestring sticks
3   hard cooked eggs
¼   teaspoon pepper
    Salt to taste
½   teaspoon crumbled oregano
    Mayonnaise

Cook vegetables in separate pans with salt according to directions on package. Arrange lettuce on salad plate. Marinate 3 or 4 of the vegetables (or more if you desire) separately in French dressing, and arrange in triangular mounds on the lettuce. Mark the divisions be-tween mounds of vegetables with asparagus spears, celery sticks or carrot sticks. Peel hardcooked eggs and press through a ricer or sieve, or chop very fine. Sprinkle over vege-tables. Place a generous dab of mayonnaise in center and top with a sprinkle of paprika and minced chives. These may be served on indi-vidual salad plates, or on one large platter from which guests serve themselves. Homemade natural yogurt is a national dish and can be substituted for the mayonnaise.

POACHED GINGER PEARS

¾   cup unsweetened pineapple juice
1   tablespoon brown sugar
2   firm pears, peeled, quartered, and cored
1   teaspoon grated lime rind
½   teaspoon ground ginger
2   tablespoons chopped almonds
    Dash of nutmeg

In a small saucepan, combine all but the pears and almonds. Bring to a boil. Add the pears and poach in the fluid until they become transparent. Do not overcook. Pears should be firm. Chill the pears in the juice. Serve in indi-vidual dishes and sprinkle with chopped al-monds just before serving.

Variations: Substitute ½ teaspoon cinna-mon, curry powder, or allspice for the ginger. Substitute ¾ cup orange or grapefruit juice for the pineapple juice. Substitute 2 quartered peaches (53 calories) or apples (72 calories) for the pears. As rich as it tastes, this is a low-calorie dessert. It serves 4.

CANADA

Stuffed Green Peppers
Cottage Cheese and Fresh Fruit
with Lemon-Honey Dressing
Orange Sandwich Bread
Apple Pie Supreme or
Ginger Ice Cream
Hot Tea

STUFFED GREEN PEPPERS

4 firm fresh green peppers
1 can (2¼ oz.) stems and pieces of mushrooms
1 cup tiny torn pieces of bread crumbs or 1 cup fluffy boiled rice
1 small white onion, chopped
1 tablespoon minced parsley
   Salt and pepper to taste
2 chopped hardboiled eggs
1 bouillon cube in ¾ cup hot water

Select the firmest well-shaped green peppers; wash and cut out a 1-inch piece from the top (stem end). Scoop out the seeds carefully, making certain that all fiber is also removed, using your fingers if necessary to prevent cutting into outer shell. Allow cold water to run inside of peppers to bring out the rest of the seeds. Drain well.

Parboil peppers in boiling water, covered, for only 10 minutes. They should not get too soft for filling. Stand each pepper up in an oiled baking pan to cool.

Sauté the drained mushrooms and onion until onion is tender and clear then blend in all the other ingredients. With a small spoon fill the green peppers. Add to the baking dish the ¾ cup of bouillon and place pan in oven at 400° for 1 hour. For other meals, these stuffed peppers can be served with a tomato sauce. Serves 4.

COTTAGE CHEESE WITH FRESH FRUIT

¼ lb. of small curd cottage cheese
1 tablespoon chopped crystallized ginger
   Fresh watercress
2 bunches seedless green grapes
1 fresh pear, sliced
1 banana, sliced

Mix chopped ginger crystals with cottage cheese. Mound on a bed of fresh watercress, and surround with grapes and slices of fresh apple or banana which have been tossed with several tablespoons of lemon-honey salad dressing.

LEMON-HONEY DRESSING

¼ cup safflower oil
2 tablespoons lemon juice
1 tablespoon honey
1 teaspoon salt

Mix together. Makes ⅔ cup of dressing. Especially good with Cottage Cheese and Fruit Salad. Serve with Orange Bread.

ORANGE SANDWICH BREAD

3 cups flour
4 teaspoons baking powder
1½ teaspoons salt
1 egg
½ cup sugar
½ cup chopped walnuts
1½ cups milk
1 cup candied orange peel, sliced

Commercially candied orange peel satisfactory for this recipe can be purchased already sliced.

Sift the flour, baking soda, salt and sugar together; add the unbeaten egg and the milk. Stir the liquids quickly and lightly into the dry ingredients, then add the nuts. Pour the batter into a loaf pan approximately 9" x 5" which has been well-greased and dusted with flour. Bake in a moderate oven (350°) for about one hour. The bread is done when the crust is brown and no particles stick to a wire cake-tester or a toothpick thrust into the center of the loaf. Loosen the loaf from the pan with a knife; remove the loaf from the pan and cool it on a wire rack. The bread should not be sliced until it is thoroughly cooled.

APPLE PIE SUPREME

Pastry:
2 level cups sifted all-purpose flour
2 teaspoons baking powder
1 cup butter or shortening (not margarine)
2 tablespoons sugar
¼ teaspoon salt
2 tablespoons cold water

Sift flour, baking powder, salt and sugar together. Cut in the shortening until it forms crumbs the size of a pea. Add very cold water drop by drop, stirring constantly until mixture becomes a ball following fork around bowl. Scrape from sides and mix with the ball. Turn out on pastry cloth or floured board and divide into two parts. Roll out one half to a circle 2 inches larger than the pan. Lift into pan and smooth out, making a few holes for air to escape to prevent large bubbles forming. Repeat with the other dough after filling has been put in bottom crust, and use for top crust.

Filling:

1 quart green cooking apples, peeled, cored and sliced
1 cup sugar
1 teaspoon sifted flour
½ teaspoon cinnamon
¼ teaspoon nutmeg
3 tablespoons water

A tip for beginning bakers is to precook the apples in a little water and sugar. After stewing apples, let them cool and then chill them for a bit. Place chilled apples and juice with seasonings in bottom crust. Put top crust lightly over them and press the edges of the top and bottom crusts together, trimming off the excess.

With your fingers or a fork, press or pinch crusts around edge of pan. With fork, make air-hole design in top crust. Place pie in center of oven shelf and bake at 450° for 15 minutes and reduce heat to 325° and continue to bake for 15 to 25 minutes longer for fruit to cook. If you have stewed your apples ahead of time, just watch for the crust to be golden, not brown, and remove from oven. Serve with ice cream or a small triangle or cube of cheddar cheese.

GINGER REFRIGERATOR ICE CREAM

4 egg yolks
2 cups milk
⅓ cup sugar
⅛ teaspoon salt
1 teaspoon pure vanilla
½ pint heavy cream, whipped
½ cup chopped preserved ginger and syrup

First make a custard by scalding the milk in the top of a double boiler. Put egg yolks in a bowl and add the sugar and salt, mixing thoroughly. Then pour the scalded milk into the egg yolks, stirring constantly while adding. Wash out the double boiler in which the milk was scalded and then return the custard, through a strainer, into the pan. Keep the water in the bottom pan just below the boiling point or the custard will curdle. Now replace the top pan on the water pan and stir slowly until the custard thickens and becomes creamy. Remember, it will not be as thick when hot as it will when you chill it. The mixture should be perfectly smooth and like fairly thin cream. In case it should curdle, remove top pan from the boiler immediately and place it in another larger pan of cold water and beat with a rotary egg beater. It will then become smooth again, do not return to heat, chill it. When the custard is cold, add the vanilla and chopped preserved ginger, and, as this is like French Vanilla Ice Cream, therefore the whipped cream is added before freezing. Fold in ½ pint of stiffly beaten whipped cream and freeze. Reserve the syrup to serve over the ice cream after it has been frozen. Makes 1 Quart.

CHINESE/CANTONESE

"Chow Dep Suey" — Snow peas with mushrooms, carrots, and water chestnuts
"Kwong-Chow Yong Don" — Egg Foo Yong
"Hong-Shu Dow-Foo" — Bean Curd fried with Mushrooms
"Soo-Moy Ding" — "Duck Sauce"
Lichee and Avocado Salad
Cantonese Sauce
Raw Carrot Salad
Rice
"Heong-Yen Beng"   Almond Cookies
Tea   Kumquats   Oriental Sundae Sauce

In Chinese meals the number of guests suggests the number of dishes to be served. Thus, if you have 5 people to serve, not less than 6 dishes should be served; for two, at least 3 dishes should be prepared. They also plan menus for variety of tastes—sweet, sour, bland, piquant—and for textures and colors as well. The variations are endless because the mixtures can be so varied. The preparation of foods is most important. Everything is chopped to bite size because no knives are used by diners. Foods are chopped and diced and arranged in small heaps to be added to the dish in the proper time; these foods cannot be cooking while you are readying the next ingredient, so all must be ready before the cooking actually begins. They have learned that vegetables are much tastier when chopped or sliced diagonally, rather than straight through. And of course rice prepared the Oriental way is always served. Never use the quick rices (which do not turn out consistently fluffy servings) with Chinese meals. Use the long cooking kind and when it is done, it should be able to be picked up with chopsticks—light but slightly sticky.

"CHOW DEP SUEY" — 2 TO 5 VEGETABLES

Basic Recipe

1   pound fresh snow peas (in pod)
1   clove garlic, peeled and pressed (or garlic powder)
4   tablespoons peanut or vegetable oil
1   level teaspoon sugar
    Thin slices of ginger root (or ½ teaspoon crushed ginger)
1   cup celery, threaded and chopped
1   raw carrot, peeled and thinly sliced
1   teaspoon light soy sauce
2   scallions, finely minced (white part only)
1   teaspoon cornstarch
1   pound fresh mushrooms (or equivalent in canned mushrooms)

1 small can water chestnuts, drained and sliced

Put oil in very heavy skillet or wok and add the scallions, garlic, sugar, ginger, cornstarch mixed in 1 teaspoon water from cooking rice, mushrooms, raw carrot, soy sauce and chestnuts. Stir-fry 2 minutes. Add whole, unshelled snow peas; toss ingredients together, cover and cook 2 minutes. [NOTE: Following this basic recipe, any number of dishes can be made. Instead of snow peas, use mustard greens, spinach, green peas, celery, onions, green pepers, Chinese or American cabbage. If broccoli or asparagus is used, cut diagonally in small pieces and cook in boiling water for 5 minutes. If over 1 pound of vegetables is used, make more sauce in proportion.]

EGG FOO YONG
("Kwong-Chow Yong Don")

8 eggs, beaten
1 teaspoon seasoning powder
1 teaspoon salt
1 cup mushrooms, black or white, shredded
½ teaspoon pepper
1 teaspoon garlic powder
3 cups bean sprouts
2 scallions, chopped (white part only)

Blend eggs, seasonings, mushrooms. Pour 3 tablespoons vegetable oil in very hot heavy skillet or wok; add bean sprouts, stir-fry 1 minute. Add 1 cup vegetarian broth (from bouillon cube), cover and cook 3 minutes. Add prepared egg mixture and chopped scallions, then press flat with spatula. Fry until one side is golden; turn and fry other side. Serve hot in Chinese dish with steamed rice, Chinese pre-serves in a small white lotus bowl, almond cookies, and tea. Chinese, or green, tea is sipped during the whole meal. The Chinese drink tea instead of water morning, noon and night.

If you have no bean sprouts you can use snow pea pods, available in frozen packages, or asparagus or any of the vegetables mentioned in the "NOTE" of Chow Dep Suey Basic Recipe. Have soy sauce on the table; Cantonese cooking is delicate and needs no extra condiment such as the soy sauce. Preserved kumquats can be purchased in markets, but if you cannot get them you can always serve chunks of pineapple instead. If you use dried mushrooms, black or white, soak them in cold water for 3 hours, drain and shred.

BEAN CURD, FRIED, WITH MUSHROOMS ("Hong-Shu Dow-Foo")

6 cakes bean curd
1½ cups mushrooms, black or white, shredded (soak black mushrooms in warm water 15 minutes)
1 teaspoon light soy sauce
1 teaspoon sugar
1 teaspoon seasoning powder
1 teaspoon salt
Pinch of pepper
½ cup water
1 tablespoon cornstarch
½ teaspoon heavy soy sauce

Cut bean cakes into 4 pieces each, fry in deep peanut oil until light golden brown. Put in deep plate. Mix light soy sauce, sugar, seasoning powder; stir well before using. Mix ½ cup water, cornstarch and ½ teaspoon heavy soy sauce together. Soak black mushrooms in warm water 15 minutes. Add mixture of light soy sauce, sugar, seasoning powder and rice water and cook with mushrooms in frying pan 5 minutes. Add cornstarch mixture and cook slowly until it becomes translucent. Pour sauce over bean curd. Garnish with fresh chopped parsley. Serves 2. Adjust portion for added guests.

DUCK SAUCE ("Soo-Moy Ding")

4   cups fresh plums, skins and stones removed, mashed
3   cups fresh apricots (or cooked dried apricots)
2   cups apples, pears, pineapple, strawberries, or peaches
1   cup vinegar
2   cups sugar
1   cup chopped pimentos

Mash all above fruits together in a blender; add vinegar, sugar, and pimentos. Put in a large saucepan and bring to a boiling point; lower heat and let simmer 1½ hours. Preserve in airtight jar in refrigerator for about one month. When ready to use, add a little water and sugar to taste.

Duck sauce is a kind of chutney, used by the Chinese especially for roast duck. In the old days it was used for pork. Now it is used for any kind of meat, or meat substitute, or salad, or with rice. This is a very delicious sauce.

LICHEE AND AVOCADO SALAD

Lichee, the edible fruit of a tree native to China, having a hard seed and sweet pulp enclosed within a thin, brittle shell; also Lichee nut)

In Chinese market buy 1 can (1 pound) lichee nuts (chill can before opening); open, drain, save liquid; dice the lichee nuts. Cut 6 ripe avocados in halves; remove pits. Mix lichee nuts with following dressing.

Combine ¼ cup lemon juice, ¼ cup liquid drained from lichee nuts, ¼ cup salad oil, 2 tablespoons soy sauce and 2 teaspoons grated fresh ginger root. Fill avocado halves with the mixture and serve at once. Serves 12 in elegant fashion.

CANTONESE SAUCE
(used on vegetables, eggs, or salad)

4   tablespoons ketchup
½   cup peanut butter
    Sugar to taste
1   teaspoon vinegar
2   dashes hot sauce (bottled)

Mix above ingredients together with a very little water to make a paste. Cook until boiling, watch carefully. Serve in small pitcher or cruet.

RAW CARROT SALAD
(with Chinese dressing)

Grate 4 cups of scraped young raw carrots on fine side of grater. (Avoid pre-washed packaged carrots from the market. Young carrots are more succulent and appealing to the taste than old ones, which have a tendency to become woody at the center.) Selected dark green tender lettuce and crisp alfalfa sprouts can be added to salad.

Mix the following ingredients; beat well or shake in a jar.

4 tablespoons lemon juice
2 tablespoons soy sauce
2 tablespoons water
½ teaspoon ginger powder or 2 teaspoons crystalized candied ginger
½ teaspoon celery seed

This dressing is also served on cucumbers. This amount makes 9 tablespoons (about 12 calories, 3 grams carbohydrate, no protein, no fat). Serve carrot salad on a bed of lettuce or watercress, with radish roses, thin-cut cucumber for garnish.

ALMOND COOKIES
("Heong-Yen Beng")

2 eggs
¾ cup sugar
⅔ cup vegetable oil
2 teaspoons almond extract
1 tablespoon almond paste (optional)
1 teaspoon vanilla extract
2½ cups pastry flour, sifted
1 teaspoon baking powder
¼ teaspoon salt

1 tablespoon water
⅓ cup blanched almonds

Beat 1 egg well, gradually add sugar, oil, almond paste and extracts. Sift dry ingredients. Beat half into egg mixture and fold in remainder. Knead dough until smooth. Form into 1-inch balls and flatten with rolling pin or bottom of a glass until ½ inch thick.

Beat 1 egg with 1 tablespoon water and brush on cookies which have been placed on cookie sheet about 1½ inches apart. Place a whole blanched almond in the center of each cookie.

Bake in hot oven 450° F. for about 10 minutes, or until cookie starts to brown. Reduce heat to 250° F. or 300° F., and bake for 20 minutes more but watch and use your judgment about when they are done. This recipe makes good cookies, not too sweet.

KUMQUATS

This smallest member of the orange family should be washed because the rind, which is sweet, is not removed before eating. Kumquats are cut in thin slices and used as a garnish for other fruits in fruit cups. The Chinese preserve this fruit. It can be found in a syrup in jars or tins in Oriental markets. In Oriental countries kumquats are served after the meal, in tiny white lotus-shaped dessert dishes.

ORIENTAL SUNDAE SAUCE

Preserved kumquats and preserved ginger blend beautifully in this exotic sundae sauce for ice cream. Top each sundae with a few toasted almonds, if you wish.

In a pan, combine ½ cup quartered, preserved kumquats (drained and seeded) with 1½ cups syrup from the kumquats and ¼ cup sliced, preserved ginger, including some of the syrup. Bring to a boil and cook, uncovered, over medium heat for about 6 minutes or until a candy thermometer registers 215°F. Stir frequently. Cool to room temperature or chill and serve over vanilla ice cream. Makes 1 cup.

DENMARK

Danish Lunch
Danish Fruit Soup
Danish Egg Casserole with Cheese Sauce
Copenhagen Lima Beans
Asparagus Salad
Danish Custard

DANISH FRUIT SOUP

5 cups water
1 lemon, its juice and its rind cut in small strips
1 small stick cinnamon
⅓ cup minute tapioca, sago or cornstarch
2 apples, peeled, cored and sliced
15 cooked prunes, pitted
1 can (2 cups) raspberries, cherries, strawberries or plums; may use fresh or frozen of approx. equal amount
⅛ cup raisins
½ cup sugar
2 or 3 fresh peaches or apricots
Dash of salt

Heat water to boiling; add lemon juice and strips of rind. Add cinnamon, tapioca (or sago), and sliced apples. Stir constantly to prevent sticking. When apples are tender, but not mushy, add other ingredients and bring to a boil and tapioca is clear. If cornstarch is used it should be mixed with the sugar *before* adding to the liquid. Pour through a fine sieve. Be careful mixture does not stick or burn. Cool and serve in soup plates, warm, or ice cold. Serves 4.

Fruit soup is good served cold the following day, as it thickens on standing. It is also delicious made with black sour cherries, and is considered a delicacy in many countries. Sago is the pith of an East Indian and Malaysian palm used in puddings.

DANISH EGG CASSEROLE

6 hardcooked eggs
3 tablespoons butter
Few sprigs of parsley
½ lb. fresh mushrooms
1 teaspoon salt
¼ teaspoon pepper

Peel eggs and cut lengthwise. Remove the yolks carefully and mash them with a fork. Clean and mince the mushrooms. Never wash fresh mushrooms under water as it destroys their texture, simply wipe them clean with a damp cloth, cut the darkened stem ends off. Sauté the mushrooms in the butter and stir in the egg yolks and some finely minced parsley, add in the salt and pepper. Fill the egg whites with this mixture as for stuffed eggs. Arrange them in a buttered shallow, heat-resistant "au gratin" platter and cover with the cheese sauce given below.

CHEESE SAUCE

Melt 1 tablespoon butter with 2 level tablespoons flour, stirring constantly. When thick, add 1 cup finely grated imported Swiss cheese and 1 cup of milk with a dash of salt. Cook over low heat on top of stove until it bubbles. Pour over the stuffed eggs and bake in slow oven heated to 325° F. for 15 minutes. This recipe serves six.

COPENHAGEN LIMA BEANS

2 packages (10 oz. each) frozen lima beans
2 cups milk
½ cup Danish blue cheese dressing (there are several name brands sold commercially)
½ cup dry bread crumbs
2 tablespoons melted butter

Cook 2 packages of frozen lima beans (10 oz. each) in unsalted water according to package instructions. Drain. Heat the milk with the blue cheese dressing and stir until the chunks of cheese melt. Add lima beans to the mixture. Combine the dry bread crumbs with 2 tablespoons melted butter and sauté over medium heat until golden brown. Pour limas and sauce into a serving bowl, sprinkle with the crumbs and serve. Serves 6 to 8.

ASPARAGUS SALAD

If fresh green asparagus is in season, it is by far the tastiest. However, you can have asparagus salad the year round if you buy the all-green asparagus tips—not the chopped kind. Always open carefully so that you slide the asparagus out bottom first and place in open soup plate. Drain carefully so as not to break the long thin spears. Arrange crisp lettuce leaves on each salad plate and carefully divide the asparagus spears in the center. Put a strip of canned pimento across the center, or if you have sweet red peppers in season, they add texture and color as well as taste in place of the pimento. For variety you may drain a can of water chestnuts and slice each thinly and sprinkle these around the asparagus. May be served with a dab of mayonnaise topped off with a dash of paprika, or with Sauce Vinaigrette. (See Brazil for Vinaigrette Sauce recipe.)

DANISH CUSTARD

1 cup brown sugar
4 eggs, beaten
1 cup milk
¼ teaspoon salt

Place brown sugar in the top of a double boiler, making the layer of sugar as level as possible. Blend milk and beaten eggs together and stir in the salt. Pour egg-milk mixture over the brown sugar so that it is completely covered. Cook over hot water until the custard is stiff when tested with a knife, this should be about 45 minutes. Chill. When ready to serve, it can be spooned out of pan into serving dishes or you may run a warmed (not hot) table knife around the edge and turn it out onto a large shallow dish or platter. It may be served with fresh berries in season, or sliced peaches.

EGYPT

Egyptian Dinner
Creamy Cauliflower Soup
Mediterranean Salad
Baked Stuffed Eggplant
Broiled Tomatoes
Sweet Farina Pudding
Melon
Demi Tasse

CREAMY CAULIFLOWER SOUP

1 medium head snowy white cauliflower
3 chopped onions
4 tablespoons butter
4 tablespoons flour
6 cups milk
  Salt to taste
¼ teaspoon white pepper
  Croutons

Cook medium head of snowy white cauliflower in a small amount of boiling water for 15 to 20 minutes, covered, until tender. In a large saucepan, cook the chopped onions in 4 tablespoons of butter until onions are clear and tender, but do not let the butter brown. Blend in 4 tablespoons flour; add enough milk to make a thick gravy-sauce as thick as whipped cream. Drain cauliflower and chop coarsely, save liquid. Add the cooked cauliflower plus the small amount of water in which it was cooked. Once more cook until the liquid has again thickened. Salt it to taste. Serve with croutons and garnish each serving with snipped chives. It can be served in cups to start a meal, or in bowls if it is a main course as in this menu. Serves 4. (See Index for Crouton recipe.)

MEDITERRANEAN SALAD

1 pkg. (9 oz.) frozen cut beans
1 can (1 lb. 4 oz.) garbanzos or chick peas
1 pkg. frozen (10-oz.) cauliflower
1 pkg. frozen artichoke hearts
1 cup olive oil
½ cup white vinegar
1 clove garlic, minced
½ teaspoon oregano, crumbled
2 quarts salad greens such as lettuce, Romaine, chicory, and escarole
1 can (4 oz.) pitted ripe olives
1 red onion, sliced and in rings
3 tomatoes, diced
2 hardcooked eggs, sliced
¼ cup blanched almonds, sliverered
  Salt and pepper

Cook frozen vegetables in separate saucepans with salt, according to package directions. Drain garbanzos. Combine oil, vinegar, pepper, oregano. Place green beans, garbanzos, cauliflower flowerets, and artichoke hearts in separate bowls, add about 4 tablespoons of the oil and vinegar dressing to each, toss lightly and chill at least 1 hour. To serve, break the salad greens into bite size pieces and place in a large shallow bowl and toss with the remaining dressing. Arrange marinated vegetables, sliced ripe olives, fresh diced and peeled tomatoes, and strips of imitation ham or vegetarian chicken in rows on top of the mixed greens. Arrange the sliced hardcooked eggs on the top and serve immediately. Serves 8.

BAKED STUFFED EGGPLANT

1 large eggplant (2 lbs.)
1 cup finely chopped young, white onions
1 cup good white bread crumbs
1 large clove of garlic, peeled and crushed
¼ teaspoon salt
⅛ teaspoon pepper

Put whole eggplant into boiling water and boil until tender, but not too soft. Remove from water and cut carefully in halves lengthwise, using a large sharp knife. Scoop out the inside, leaving a shell ¾-inch thick, being careful not to break the skin. Heat the chopped onion in butter or oil and allow to cook until it is a golden color. Then add the scooped out, cooked chopped eggplant pulp.

Add bread crumbs, salt, pepper and crush garlic clove. Mix all ingredients together and refill the shells. Place 6 tablespoons of butter in a small baking casserole and put in the oven to melt. When hot, put in the stuffed eggplant shells, sprinkle tops with butter and bread or cracker crumbs. Return to oven and baste often with butter. If you will preheat the oven to 350° and bake for 35 to 40 minutes, the tops should be brown and bubbly. It is nice to serve each guest a half shell. If this portion seems too much, cut them into quarters. Serves 2 to 4.

BROILED TOMATOES

Select ripe but firm tomatoes. Remove stem piece, halve crosswise. Two halves for each serving so plan accordingly. Sprinkle each top with salt and a dash of pepper. Add a dab of butter and put under broiler for 10 to 12 minutes, until heated through and bubbly on top. Parmesan cheese can also be sprinkled on top. To retain juice, bake 15 minutes in 350°F. oven.

SWEET FARINA PUDDING

4 cups cold, cooked farina
2 eggs, separated
¾ cup sugar
   Butter
   Pinch of salt
   Rind of 1 whole lemon, grated

This traditional Middle Eastern dessert is a sweet farina pudding enjoyed by young and old.

Mix sugar well with the farina. Add yolks of 2 eggs, sugar and salt. Next stir in the grated rind of 1 lemon. Beat the egg whites until stiff and fold in carefully until blended with the farina mixture. Pour into a buttered baking dish, dot with butter and bake in oven set and preheated to 350°F. until it rises and becomes a golden brown. Serve it with lemon sauce, see recipe given below.

44

LEMON SAUCE

1 cup sugar
½ cup boiling water
1 egg yolk
½ cup butter
   Rind and juice of one lemon

Mix butter and sugar well and add a lightly beaten egg yolk. Add the boiling water, the lemon juice and rind. Place in top of double boiler and stir while thickening over the heat. Serve hot over Sweet Farina Pudding.

PERSIAN MELON

Serve the halves of a fragrant Persian, honey dew melon or cool Casaba melon, with wedges of lemon or lime. You may want to put a scoop of pineapple, raspberry or orange sherbet in each half. Melons contain alkaline organic salts.

FINLAND

Menu
Finnish Summer Soup
Cheese Fritters
Mushrooms Pudding
Glazed Parsnips or Parsnips in Drawn Butter
Broccoli Lorraine
Paasiaisleppa (Finnish Easter Bread in a Pail)
Prune Whip or Jellied Apples with Raisins
Coffee

FINNISH SUMMER SOUP

15 tiny new carrots, scrubbed; (or 7 or 8 small carrots cut into 2 inch lengths)
1 cup sweet new shelled peas (or 1 pkg. tiny frozen peas)
2 cups tiny snap beans (or 1 10 oz. pkg. cut green beans)
3 cups new sweet onions, chopped, or 3 green onions with tops, cut in half-inch lengths
2 cups tiny new potatoes, or 2 large potatoes cut into 1-inch cubes
½ cup water
1 tablespoon sugar
½ teaspoon salt
2 tablespoons flour
4 cups light cream
2 tablespoons butter
Minced parsley

Bring to a boil in a large pot, the carrots, peas, beans, onions, potatoes, water, salt and sugar. Reduce heat, cover and simmer for 5 to 8 minutes, or until vegetables are almost tender. In a small saucepan blend the melted butter, flour and cream to make a white sauce. Pour a little of the soup liquid into the small pan to thin out the white sauce, then return all of it to the large soup pot; simmer 10 minutes. Pour into soup tureen and garnish with minced parsley. Serve immediately. Serves 6 to 8.

CHEESE FRITTERS

This is a good recipe when you have guests who are unfamiliar with vegetarian food.

2 cups milk
1 onion, peeled
1 whole clove
1 bay leaf
½ cup Semolina, a fine flour
¾ cup grated sharp cheddar cheese
1 tablespoon chopped parsley
¼ teaspoon salt
⅛ teaspoon pepper
½ teaspoon dry mustard or small pinch of cayenne
Toasted bread crumbs
1 large beaten egg

46

In a saucepan, put milk, onion, clove and bay leaf and heat almost to the boiling point. Turn off heat and allow mixture to stand for 15 minutes. Remove the onion, clove and bay leaf. Reheat milk to boiling and sprinkle Semolina over it, stirring constantly. Simmer gently for about 2 minutes. Remove from heat and beat in the grated cheese, seasonings and parsley. Spread the mixture smoothly over a wet plate or board, and smooth the surface with a rubber scraper. Allow to get cold. With a knife, cut into 8 pieces; dip each piece into beaten egg and then into the bread crumbs. Fry in hot salad oil or vegetable shortening until crisp and golden. Drain well on paper towels to absorb the grease. These can be fried ahead of time, then before serving placed on a baking sheet in an oven heated to 350° to heat through for serving. Serves 4, allowing 2 per person.

GLAZED PARSNIPS

12 parsnips
4 tablespoons butter
4 tablespoons brown sugar

Scrub and scrape the parsnips. If young, slice them in rounds, if mature, cut them once lengthwise and once across, quartering them, and remove the core if they are woody. Cook in covered saucepan in a very small amount of boiling salted water for 10 minutes. Drain and arrange in a buttered pie pan or shallow baking dish. Spread with butter and sprinkle with brown sugar. Bake in oven preheated to 375° for 25 minutes, or until glazed. Or you might prefer to serve parsnips prepared the following way.

PARSNIPS IN DRAWN BUTTER

12 parsnips
2 teaspoons sugar
8 tablespoons butter
4 tablespoons flour
1 tablespoon lemon juice
   Pinch of salt

Scrape the parsnips and allow to cook in a little boiling salted water for about 15 minutes, if left whole, less if sliced. Add about 2 teaspoons sugar. In a saucepan, melt 4 tablespoons butter and add 4 tablespoons flour; blend and gradually add the liquid saved from the parsnips, stirring constantly to prevent lumping or burning. Cook until sauce thickens, about 5 minutes. Add 1 tablespoon lemon juice, a pinch of salt, and 4 tablespoons butter. Stir well and blend, and add the drained parsnips. Serves 6.

** Parsnips are rich in calcium and contain starch and sugar, having a high fuel value. Calcium (lime) builds bones and teeth, coagulates the blood, aids in regulating the mineral metabolism. It is the "master mineral". Vitamin D must be included to make calcium available, as without it, calcium fats irradiated in the sun are sources of Vitamin D. It is found in parsnips, carrots, cauliflower, legumes, green vegetables, citrus fruits, almonds, molasses, cheese, and soy bean milk, the latter contains calcium oxide.

MUSHROOM PUDDING (Sirniki)

2 cups milk
2½ cups bread cubes
6 tablespoons butter
2 pounds fresh mushrooms
1 cup chopped onion
4 egg yolks, beaten
4 egg whites beaten to a peak
1½ teaspoons salt
¼ teaspoon pepper
3 tablespoons minced parsley
2 tablespoons dry bread crumbs

Soak bread cubes in the milk until soft, then mash thoroughly. Melt 3 tablespoons butter in skillet and sauté the cleaned mushrooms 5 minutes and remove to a bowl. Melt the remaining butter and sauté onions in it for 10 minutes. Mix the mashed bread cubes, mushrooms, onion, egg yolks, pepper and parsley. Carefully fold in the beaten egg whites. Turn into a buttered 1½-quart straight-sided casserole and sprinkle with bread crumbs and dot the top with butter. Set casserole in a shallow pan with 1 inch of water. Bake at 350°F. for 50 minutes or until browned on top. Serve immediately. Makes 4 servings.

BROCCOLI LORRAINE

1½ pounds broccoli
⅛ teaspoon nutmeg
4 eggs, lightly beaten
1½ cups light cream
¾ teaspoon salt
⅛ teaspoon pepper
½ teaspoon dry mustard
3 tablespoons freshly grated Parmesan cheese

Place stems of broccoli in boiling water for 5 minutes. Add the flowerettes and boil 2 minutes longer, or until tender. Drain well and turn into a 2-quart shallow baking dish. In a bowl combine ¾ teaspoon salt, the nutmeg, pepper and dry mustard and add the lightly beaten eggs. Stir in cream and add the Parmesan cheese. Pour this mixture over the broccoli. Set the baking dish in a larger pan with about ¼ of an inch of water in it. Bake at 350°F. for 25- to 30 minutes or until it is set (when you shake the dish back and forth only a 3-inch circle in the center moves). Serve at once. This recipe serves 6.

PRUNE WHIP

2 cups strained prunes (or 2 jars baby food prunes)
½ cup prune juice
1 cup boiling water
1 cup brown sugar
¼ teaspoon cinnamon
⅛ teaspoon salt
2 tablespoons cornstarch
¼ cup cold water
1 tablespoon lemon juice
½ cup chopped walnuts (optional)
2 egg whites, beaten stiff
½ cup heavy cream, whipped

Combine prunes, prune juice, boiling water, sugar, cinnamon, and salt. Mix the cornstarch and cold water until smooth and stir into the prune mixture. Cook over low heat, stirring constantly until mixture reaches the boiling point. Cook five minutes longer, stirring occasionally. Cool and stir in the lemon juice, and the walnuts if you want them. Fold in the beaten egg whites and whipped cream. Pour into individual serving dishes. Chill and garnish with a dab of whipped cream.

JELLIED APPLES WITH RAISINS

1 envelope agar-agar (seaweed)/lemon
　flavored gelatin
1¼ cups boiling water
2 apples
2 tablespoons raisins
　Whipped cream
　Vanilla

Grate apples coarsely and mix with raisins. Make the gelatin with 1¼ teaspoons agar-agar. (The advantage of this gelatin is that it sets much more quickly than gelatin made from animal tissue, and that it also adds useful minerals. One teaspoonful will set half a pint of liquid.) Mix with hot water and stir until dissolved. Divide the liquid into four glass dessert dishes, and allow to set. Serve topped with whipped cream sweetened with sugar and a dash of vanilla. Serves 4.

PAASIAISLEIPA
(Finnish Easter Bread)

This aromatic sweet bread of Finland is traditionally baked in a small milk pail to symbolize abundance. The finished loaf resembles a giant mushroom. Its name—Paasiaisleipa—comes from the Finnish word meaning "to get free", which also is the root of the word for Easter. You can bake it in two pails, such as children's sand buckets (about 1½ to 2 quarts in size), or in 2-pound coffee cans. But do not use a galvanized pail!

2 pkg. yeast, active dry or compressed
½ cup warm water (lukewarm)
1½ cups light cream, scalded and cooled, or
　undiluted evaporated milk

2 cups unsifted flour
5 egg yolks
1 cup sugar
1 cup unsalted butter, melted and cooled
1½ teaspoons salt
2 teaspoons freshly ground cardamon
2 teaspoons freshly grated lemon peel
2 tablespoons grated orange peel
1 cup golden raisins
1 cup chopped blanched almonds
1 cup milk, scalded and cooled
2 cups rye flour
4 to 4½ cups unsifted all-purpose white flour

1. Dissolve yeast in the water in a large bowl. Stir in the cream and 2 cups flour, and beat until smooth. Cover and let rise in a warm place until doubled in size (½ to 1 hour).
2. Stir in the egg yolks, sugar, butter, salt, cardamon, lemon and orange peel, raisins, and almonds; beat until thoroughly combined. Stir in one cup of milk and the rye flour until combined, then stir in all but ½ cup of the remaining white flour to make a stiff dough. Sprinkle last ½ cup flour on board and turn dough out onto floured board and knead until smooth—about 10 minutes. Butter the bowl and place kneaded dough into it; turn dough over to grease top; cover lightly, and let rise until dough is doubled in size.
3. Punch dough down and work into a smooth ball. Place dough, rounded side up, in 2 well-buttered (straight-sided) 2-quart pails and let rise until dough is doubled in bulk.
4. Bake in a moderate oven (350°F.) for 1 hour.
5. Before removing from oven, test with a long straw or wooden skewer to make sure it is done all through. If the bread is well browned and sounds hollow when tapped

with finger, brush the top of loaves with butter while hot and let cool in the pail for about 20 minutes before turning out onto a wire rack. Cool completely. Cut loaf in quarters and slice, making about 40 triangular slices from the two loaves. It is delicious with soft cheeses such as Camembert, Brie, or natural cream cheese. Hard cheeses such as Edam, Swiss or Gouda are also excellent when bread is accompaniments with Summer Soup.

FRANCE

Since French cuisine is the basis of fine cooking the world over, and since so many of the recipes used in other countries have derived from basic French cuisine, I have not offered one sample menu. Rather, I have offered you some of the basic recipes for which France is so famous, and from which so many variations can be made. These then can be used in the culinary arts of many countries and many menus in many ways.

Basic Vegetable Broth
Mayonnaise
Vichyssoise
Cheese Soufflé
Crêpes and Fillings

Hollandaise Sauce
French Onion Soup
Quiche Lorraine
Croissants
Croutons

BASIC VEGETABLE BROTH (Soup Stock)

4 onions, chopped coarsely
4 carrots, diced
4 ribs celery with leaves, chopped coarsely
4 parsnips, diced
2 turnips, peeled and diced
4 tablespoons oil or butter
⅓ cup dried parsley
2 teaspoons pepper corns
2 bay leaves
½ teaspoon basil
½ teaspoon thyme
3½ teaspoons salt
3 quarts water

In large kettle, sauté onions, carrots, celery, parsnips and turnips in oil or butter until tender, about 15 minutes. Tie parsley, peppercorns, bay leaves, basil and thyme in a piece of cheesecloth about 6 inches square. Add the bag of seasonings to the kettle with salt and water and bring to a boil; cover and lower the heat and simmer for 3 hours. Strain broth. Use as a base for sauces, soups, or for cooking grains such as buckwheat kernels or rice. This broth is good as a first course or as a light meal with fresh baked bread and cheese. If desired, you can pureé the vegetables or press through a sieve with the back of a spoon, then add back into the broth.

HOLLANDAISE SAUCE

2 egg yolks
2 teaspoons lemon juice
¼ teaspoon salt
2 half eggshells of cold water*
2 tablespoons melted butter
   Few grains of pepper

In the top of a double boiler put egg yolks, salt, cold water, and lemon juice; whisk to a froth. Place over the boiling water in the bottom half of pan, and whisk hard all the time, until thick and pale yellow, about 2 or 3 minutes. Add the two tablespoons of melted butter, beating steadily. When thoroughly blended, remove from heat. This recipe can be increased by doubling or tripling the amounts. Proportions should always remain the same. Hollandaise is particularly delicious on vegetable dishes such as asparagus on toast, over broccoli, spinach, and others.

* When breaking eggs and separating them, save one of the eggshell halves to measure the water.

MAYONNAISE

- 1 teaspoon salt
- 1 teaspoon paprika
- 1 teaspoon dry mustard
- 2 egg yolks
- 1 cup olive oil (cold pressed) important for flavor
- 1 tablespoon lemon juice
- 1 tablespoon malt or tarragon vinegar
- 1 tablespoon boiling water

Use a small bowl that will hold about 2 cups of liquid. In it mix salt, paprika and dry mustard. Add egg yolks and mix well with a rotary egg beater or electric mixer. Now comes the tip that will solve all your mayonnaise problems: Add 1 tablespoon of boiling water and beat again! Add the oil about 1 tablespoon at a time, beating well after each addition so to completely combine the oil with the other ingredients. Repeat until most of the oil is used and then you can add the oil faster. Add lemon juice and vinegar last. The mayonnaise keeps well if tightly covered in the refrigerator. Prepare the day before using.

FRENCH ONION SOUP

- Butter for sautéing
- 8 medium or 4 large Spanish Onions
- 3¼ quarts (26 cups) boiling water
- ½ teaspoon per cup of water or any good vegetarian bouillon paste - a total of 13 teaspoons

Cut onions into slices and cross cut the slices. Sauté onions in a skillet or pot. Be sure to lower the flame and allow onions to slowly simmer for about 10 minutes, turning them at least twice. Watch carefully and do not allow them to brown but let them cook until soft. To 3¼ quarts of boiling water (26 cups) add 13 teaspoons of vegetarian bouillon paste or make bouillon with vegetarian cubes, to make this broth. Add the sautéed onions to this boiling bouillon and allow to cook for 5 minutes longer.

Trim very thin slices of bread, cut into circles and toast one per serving. Place one slice of toast in each serving bowl and ladle the steaming soup over it. Pass the diners freshly grated Parmesan or Gruyère cheese to sprinkle in the soup. Serve piping hot.

CROUTONS

Cut bread into thin sticks, then cut sticks into cubes. The slices may be spread with soft butter or dipped, before cutting, into melted butter in the frying pan. Place cubes on a cookie sheet to toast, but watch them closely to keep them from burning. For larger croutons cut bread into quarters, then cut each square diagonally into triangles. Turn or shake to brown all over.

Add croutons to soup or sprinkle over green salads.

VICHYSSOISE

4   leeks
4   potatoes, large size
5   tablespoons butter
1   cup cream
    chopped chives

Select fresh, green firm leeks, do not buy wilted ones. Wash thoroughly, separating the green part to let water run through. Cut the stem end and the green tops from the leeks, and slice the stalks into 1-inch pieces. Sauté slowly in 5 tablespoons of butter; do not substitute margarine or you will not get the flavor famous in vichyssoise. In a heavy saucepan, continue cooking the leeks until yellow, about 5 minutes. Add the 4 potatoes, sliced thin, and about 6 cups boiling water. Simmer for about 20 minutes. Rub the leeks and potatoes through a sieve or use a blender to completely mash, then return to liquid and add one cup of cream. Add salt to taste. If you want to stretch the amount of soup, add thin cream, never use water. Garnish the top of vichyssoise with a sprinkle of finely chopped chives. Although the French like their vichyssoise served hot as other soups, it is mostly served chilled in the United States. It can be chilled in a tureen, adding the chives just before serving, or they can be sprinkled on the individual bowls as served. This is delicious served with a glob of sour cream, as in Normandy.

QUICHE LORRAINE (pronounced KEESH)

This hot, crusty cheese custard is from the Alsace and Lorraine districts.

1   unbaked 9-inch pie shell
½   pound Swiss cheese (natural) grated
1½ cups heavy whipping cream
½   cup light cream
4   eggs
½   teaspoon salt
    Tiny pinch of cayenne pepper
¼   teaspoon nutmeg, freshly grated
1   tablespoon chopped green onion, white part only
    A few grains of Cayenne

Distribute 1½ cups grated Swiss cheese on the bottom of the pastry shell. Do not use processed cheese when the natural product is called for. Blend by beating together the whipping cream, light cream, eggs, salt and the few grains of cayenne. Last add the finely minced spoon of onion.

Pastry for Shell

1 cup sifted white flour (important)
1 teaspoon baking powder
1 tablespoon granulated sugar
1 tablespoon of cold water
⅛ teaspoon salt
¼ pound unsalted, sweet butter
   (no substitute)

It is important that there be no cracks in the pastry shell. Sift the flour *before* measuring. Resift the flour together with the baking powder, sugar and salt. Into this add the butter and work to a fine crumble with a pastry blender. Do not over mix. The butter pieces should be no larger than a marble, when it has been sufficiently and properly blended. Add a drop of water at a time, cutting it through the mixture with a spatula, turning it over to bring dry particles to the top. Add water to dry particles only. When there are no more dry spots, push the dough together; form into a ball with the hands. Be sure to use all the scraps in the mixing bowl. Roll dough out on a pastry cloth or lightly floured piece of wax paper. Place dough in the center. Sift a little flour over the rolling pin and the dough then roll to two inches larger than pie pan. Lift carefully into the pan making certain there are no cracks in it.

Pour quiche filling into shell and bake at 375° for 40 minutes, or until firm when shaken gently. Serve warm, not hot. Allow to stand 20 minutes. This is an entrée and is "delicieux - Bon appétit." Serves 6.

CHEESE SOUFFLÉ, BAKED IN TOMATOES

You will find a number of different soufflé recipes throughout this book and all are, essentially, French. The high-rising, top puffed soufflé is an entree, a dessert, an accompliment to other foods. This following recipe is a charming variation.

12 firm tomatoes
 3 tablespoons butter
 2 tablespoons flour
   Salt and pepper
½ cup light cream
 6 eggs, separated
1¾ cups Swiss cheese (7 oz.) grated

Slice off the tomato tops and scoop out the pulp but do not break the shells. Sprinkle with salt and pepper. Melt the butter and stir in the flour. Gradually add the cream plus 3 of the egg yolks. Season mixture with about ½ teaspoon of salt and ¼ teaspoon pepper. Cook over low heat, stirring constantly, until it is smooth and thickened. Remove from heat. Beat in the grated cheese and the remaining 3 egg yolks. Cool the mixture. Beat the egg whites until they are stiff and fold them into the egg and cheese mixture. Spoon into the tomatoes, filling each about ¾ full. Place the tomatoes in a buttered shallow baking dish. Set in oven preheated to 350° and bake for 15 to 20 minutes, making certain that the soufflé has risen and become golden brown. As a main dish, serve two per guest and serve immediately upon removing from oven.

FABULOUS, EASY CRÊPES
Crêpe Batter:

3 eggs
2 tablespoons salad oil
¾ cup sifted flour
½ teaspoon salt
1 cup milk
  Butter

Beat the eggs, milk, salt and salad oil together. Stir in the flour.

Heat a little butter or oil in a 6-inch skillet. Pour about 2 tablespoons of the batter into it, tilting the pan to thinly coat the bottom. Use just enough batter to make a very thin pancake. Let the bottom brown, then carefully turn out onto a napkin, browned side up. Watch the heat carefully, as the batter burns easily.

Spread 1 heaping tablespoon of any of the fillings along one side of the crêpe, then turn opposite sides in and roll up like a jelly roll.

As each crêpe is finished, slip it onto a plate. You can either fill each pancake as it is done or stack them and fill together afterward. During the preparation, the crêpes will probably cool enough so you will have to reheat them before serving. Because they are so thin, they reheat rapidly. Most stacks of crêpes will heat through in no more than 10 to 20 minutes in a very moderate oven. It is a good idea to make them ahead of time and heat and fill them just before serving. Crêpes also keep well if completely covered and refrigerated for a day or so, or they can be frozen, thawed and reheated to fill. Makes about 18 crêpes.

DINNER CRÊPE FILLINGS
Cheese Filling

2 cups drained cottage cheese, small curd
1 egg yolk
¾ teaspoon salt
1 tablespoon melted butter
2 tablespoons sugar (optional)
1 teaspoon lemon juice (optional)

Beat the cheese, egg yolk, salt and butter together. Add sugar or lemon juice if you like since some like them sweet and some do not. Place on crêpe and roll.

Spinach Filling

4 cups well-drained, chopped spinach, cooked
2 tablespoons butter
2 teaspoons flour
½ cup heavy cream

Either fresh, frozen or canned spinach can be used. For frozen or fresh spinach, drain completely and proceed as follows. Melt butter in a wide frying pan over highest heat, add 4 cups of lightly packed spinach, stirring until liquid is evaporated. Sprinkle spinach with 2 teaspoons flour and mix well. Add ½ cup of heavy (whipping) cream and continue to cook and stir over high heat until cream is bound with spinach and there is no freely flowing liquid. Season with salt to taste. Use one heaping tablespoon per crêpe. Makes at least 8 crêpes.

DESSERT CRÊPE FILLINGS

Cheese Filling

1 package cream cheese (8 oz.), softened
¼ cup butter, unsalted
⅓ cup sugar
1 teaspoon grated lemon peel
3 tablespoons golden raisins

Spread crêpes evenly with the cheese mixture and roll each one, folding the ends to completely enclose the filling. Arrange the folded crêpes side by side in a buttered baking dish (about 11 x 17 inches). Pour over them as much heavy whipping cream (not whipped) as they will absorb—about 1 cup. Bake in a moderate oven, 350°, for 10 minutes or until heated through. Makes 12 crêpes.

Orange Cheese Filling and Sauce

⅔ cup good orange marmalade
1 teaspoon lemon juice
1 4-oz. package of cream cheese, softened

In a small saucepan, heat a scant ⅔ cup of best available orange marmalade with lemon juice. Set aside for use as sauce. Beat 2 tablespoons marmalade into the softened cream cheese. Spoon about 1 tablespoon into each crêpe and roll up. Place 2 per serving on a plate and pour sauce over them.

Let your own originality guide you to making up crêpe fillings and sauces. Makes 6 crêpes.

FRENCH CROISSANTS (Crescent Rolls)

Although croissants can now be bought in the frozen section of many American food markets, everyone loves the flaky, tender real French croissants. The classic method of preparation takes patience and time. Following is a *simplified* version of the famous original great recipe.

1 cake or package of yeast
¼ cup lukewarm water
¾ cup milk
½ cup butter
4 tablespoons sugar
1 teaspoon salt
3 eggs, beaten
4½ cups sifted flour

Soften the yeast in the lukewarm water. Scald the milk and stir in the softened butter, sugar and salt. Cool to lukewarm. Stir in the yeast, eggs and flour. Knead until smooth dough is formed. Place in a greased bowl and cover. Let the dough rise until it has doubled in bulk.

Divide the dough in thirds and roll each piece into a 10-inch circle. Cut each circle into 12 wedge-shaped pieces. Roll up each wedge, beginning with the large end up to the point, which should be on top. Place these rolled wedges which you slightly curve in at the ends, on a greased baking pan or sheet. They should be placed several inches apart in their crescent shapes. Let them rise again until doubled in bulk, then brush with melted butter.

Bake in oven preheated to 400°F. for 15 minutes or until browned. Makes about 36 croissants.

GERMANY /Bavaria
Cold Weather Dinner
Weisse Kartoffelsuppe - (German Potato-Carrot Soup)
Baviere Kasepudding - (Bavarian Cheese Pudding)
Pfifferling Salat (German Mushroom Salad)　　Braised Kale
Robes Apfelmus (Uncooked Applesauce)　　Pumpernickel Bread
Chriesitotsch (Baked Cherry Pudding)
Coffee Bavarian Cream

GERMAN POTATO AND CARROT SOUP
("Weisse Kartoffelsuppe")

9　potatoes
3　onions, finely chopped
3　carrots, grated
6　tablespoons butter
1　pint sour cream
6　tablespoons flour
4　tablespoons chopped parsley
　　Salt & white pepper
2½　quarts of milk (10 cups)

Boil potatoes in salted water, starting in cold water. Cook with lid on pot. Put butter in frying pan over fire. When golden brown, add the finely chopped onion and carrots, and turn flame down under pan, or move on stove to where it will not cook too fast. Allow to slowly cook for twenty minutes; then sift in the six tablespoons of flour and stir to thoroughly blend. When adding flour to hot liquids, it is best to make a thin paste of the flour in small amount of cold water, then mix it more with hot liquid from pan before putting it into the pot; in this way you avoid lumps. When blended add slowly about 1 cup of milk, stirring while adding. Then pour the contents of the frying pan into a saucepan and add the rest of the milk. Mash 6 of the boiled potatoes (through a ricer or sieve) and cut the other 3 potatoes into very small pieces. Add the potatoes (both mashed and cut up) to the other ingredients in the pot. Add the parsley and season to taste. Allow to simmer for a few minutes after the parsley and seasoning are added. Garnish with sour cream. Reheats perfectly.

The Germans add about 1 teaspoon of vinegar to this soup, not to make the soup sour, but to give it a particularly smooth, silky consistency. It does improve the soup and you might like to try it.

Good served with a tossed salad and any natural cheese.

GERMAN MUSHROOM SALAD
("Pfifferling salat")

1 cup pfifferling (German mushrooms)
1 medium onion, minced
1 tablespoon parsley, chopped
1 tablespoon salad oil
  Salt & pepper to taste
1 tablespoon vinegar
1 teaspoon sugar
1 German pickle, diced
¾ tomatoes, peeled and diced

Combine onion, parsley with vinegar, oil and sugar, beat lightly. Add pickle, tomatoes, and mushrooms to marinade and stir gently. Season with salt and pepper to taste.

BAVARIAN CHEESE PUDDING

("Baviere Kasepudding")

4 eggs, separated
2 cups heavy cream
1 cup grated Swiss cheese
½ teaspoon salt
6 slices firm white bread
¼ cup melted butter

Beat the egg yolks. Mix with the cream, cheese, and salt. Beat the egg whites until stiff; fold into the egg yolk mixture. Sauté the bread in the heated butter on both sides until golden. Butter a 9x9-inch baking dish and arrange in it overlapping slices of bread. Pour the cheese mixture over the bread and place the baking dish in a pan of warm water in a pre-heated 350°F oven. Bake for 35 to 40 minutes or until pudding is golden brown and puffed. Serve immediately. Serves 4.

BRAISED KALE

3 pounds kale
4 tablespoons butter
1 clove garlic, minced
3 tablespoons water
⅛ teaspoon pepper
1 teaspoon potato flour
2 teaspoons lemon juice
  Salt

Wash the kale and remove the tough veins. Wash again in several changes of water. Melt butter in a saucepan and stir in the garlic, kale, water, salt and pepper. Cover and cook over low heat 15 minutes or until tender. Mix together the potato flour and lemon juice and stir into the kale. Cook 2 minutes. Serves 4.

UNCOOKED APPLESAUCE
(Robes Apfelmus)

  Juice of 3 or 4 lemons
2 pounds firm apples
  Sugar or honey to taste
½ cup heavy cream

Put the lemon juice into a bowl. Stem and core the apples, but do not peel them. Grate the apples directly into the lemon juice. As they should not discolor, keep stirring the lemon juice over them. Sweeten to taste with honey or sugar. Fold in the whipped cream and serve immediately.

BAKED CHERRY PUDDING
(Chriesitotsch)

6 tablespoons butter
7 tablespoons sugar
4 eggs, separated
½ cup blanched almonds,
    finely ground
1 lemon rind grated
1 cup zwieback finely grated
1 cup either milk, or cream, or juice drained
    from cherries
2 cups pitted black cherries, drained

Cream butter with sugar and cream; beat until frothy. Egg yolks are added one at a time, beating well after each addition. In a blender grind the almonds to which grated lemon rind, zwieback crumbs and cream are added. Blend; fold in stiffly beaten whites of eggs. Pour half of the batter into a well-buttered 8-inch spring form pan. Bake in a preheated 350 degree oven for 10 minutes. Remove from the oven and top with the drained cherries and the remaining batter. Continue baking at same temperature for an additional 20 to 30 minutes or until golden and firm. Serve hot with cream.

COFFEE BAVARIAN CREAM

1 tablespoon vegetarian gelatin (made with
    tapioca or agar-agar seaweed)
½ cup cold water
¼ cup sugar
1¼ cups strong coffee
½ teaspoon vanilla extract
⅓ cup heavy whipping cream

Put gelatin in top of double boiler, pour in cold water; let stand at room temperature 5 to 10 minutes; add sugar. Stir over boiling water until dissolved. Remove from stove; add coffee and another ½ cup of water. Replace hot water in bottom part of double boiler with ice cubes. Chill until gelatin is the consistency of an unbeaten egg white. With a rotary beater, beat the jelly until light, folding into the whipped cream with the vanilla extract then beat until stiff. Pour into sherbet glasses with stems and serve with additional whipped cream on top.

GHANA (WEST AFRICA)

Characteristic Foods
Palm Soup
Nkrakra (light soup)
Peanut Soup
Jollof Rice

NOTES ON SPECIAL FOODS

Fufu is cooked cassava, plantain or yam, which is pounded in a mortar with a little water into paste. It is now quite common to find plantain in the markets; it looks like a larger greenish banana.

Banku is fermented corn meal with a little water added to it and stirred over low heat until it thickens into paste.

Kenke is fermented corn meal, about two cupfuls, each cup wrapped in aluminum foil and cooked in a pot filled to the brim with water, for forty minutes.

PALM SOUP

¾ to 1 pound Jerusalem artichokes
1   onion, medium size
1   can (16 oz.) Palm oil
3   cans (16 oz. each) water
1   large or 2 small tomatoes
12 whole okras
1   large eggplant already washed, cooked and mashed

Cut artichoke into good-sized pieces, wash and put into pot. Add chopped onion, small quantity of salt and a very small amount of water. Put the lid on the pot and boil until the moisture dries up. This gives the soup its typical flavor. Add the palm oil and the rest of the water. Bring to a boil and add the cut okra and eggplant. Cook tomatoes in a little water, blend or mash and add this pureé to the soup. Add salt and pepper to taste and boil slowly for forty to sixty minutes. Bread crumbs or toasted corn flour (meal) can be used to thicken the soup when necessary. Serve with fufu, banku, kenke, or rice. Serves six.

NKRAKRA (light soup)

1 pound mushrooms
4 tomatoes, medium sized
2 quarts cold water
1 teaspoon ground pepper
3 small onions
2 eggplants, medium size
1 teaspoon salt

Cut mushrooms into small pieces, add water, and boil slowly until tender. Add chopped eggplant and pepper and boil until tender. Add chopped onions, tomatoes, and salt, and simmer until everything is tender. Serve with banku or fufu. Serves six.

PEANUT SOUP

1 cup peanut butter
4 tomatoes, medium size
2 small eggplants
8 cups of water
½ pound spinach
1 large onion, diced
  Pepper and salt

Cut spinach into pieces. Put into cooking pot with chopped onion, salt, and a little of the water. Put on the fire. Wash and add whole, unpeeled tomatoes and eggplant; cook these until tender and remove them from the soup. Mix peanut butter with the remaining water and strain into soup. Mash the cooked tomatoes and add along with pepper. Cook all briskly for a few minutes, then reduce the heat and cook slowly for about thirty minutes. Remove skin and seeds from eggplant and return to soup, or serve separately. Serve soup hot, with fufu, cooked yam, or rice. Serves six.

JOLLOF RICE
(served in all West African countries)

3 cups uncooked long grain rice
2 tablespoons peanut oil
1 teaspoon salt
2 cups vegetable broth (see Index)
2 vegetarian bouillon cubes
2½ to 3 cups water
¼ cup peanut oil
1½ cups chopped onion
3 cups imitation ham (vegetarian)
1 can (12 oz.) whole tomatoes, diced but do not drain
½ can (6 oz.) tomato paste
2 hot dried red peppers, soaked in water and then squeezed
3 hardcooked eggs, halved
¼ cup chopped parsley

Wash rice in warm water, changing water until it is clear. Drain well. In a 4-quart saucepan, heat 2 tablespoons oil and salt. Add ¼ cup rice and brown lightly, stirring frequently. Add remaining rice, the vegetable broth and enough water to cover the rice about 1 inch. Lower the heat and simmer gently for 1 hour. In a 10-inch skillet, heat ¼ cup of peanut oil. Add the chopped onion and sauté until it is transparent. Stir in the vegetarian ham, tomatoes with their juice, and the tomato paste. Cover and cook over medium heat for 10 minutes. Drain off 1 cup of the liquid and reserve it.

Add tomato mixture and the juice from the peppers to the rice, blending it in well. Cover and cook until the tomato mixture is absorbed, about 3 minutes. If rice is too dry, add a bit of the reserved liquid as needed. Garnish with chopped parsley and slices of hardcooked eggs. Serves 8.

GREAT BRITAIN

This collection of recipes is gathered from England, Wales and Scotland—all a part of Great Britain.

— ENGLAND —

BAKED VEGETABLE MARROW (squash)

1 medium to large marrow
1 10-oz. package frozen peas
1 10-oz. package frozen corn
   Butter
1 10-oz. package pearl onions
1 cup minced celery
1 cup small jar/can mushroom caps and
   pieces
1 teaspoon crushed oregano

Wash and clean marrow, and after removing the seeds, also remove some of the meat to hollow out shells and save. Halve the marrow lengthwise, if they are very large you may want to halve them again, making 4 smaller boats. In a large saucepan, using a minimum amount of water, cook the peas, corn and celery and onions together until tender. Use more than usual the amount of salt in the water to cook, then drain them. Chopping up the marrow meat removed before, add to the mixture of vegetables then add the mushrooms and oregano. Scoop the vegetable mixture into the marrow boats and put large dots of butter on the mounds of vegetable filling. Place in shallow pan with just enough water to cover the bottom. Cover the top with foil and bake for 45 minutes to 1 hour in oven set 325°. Uncover, sprinkle the tops with grated Parmesan cheese and serve.

BRAISED OF BAKED ENDIVE OR CELERY

1 endive for each guest
1 box Zwieback
   Butter
   Salt to taste
   White pepper

Make bread crumbs of the Zwieback by placing them in a plastic bag and crushing them with a rolling pin. They can be measured as bread crumbs directly from the same plastic bag as well as being stored in it.

Butter individual baking dishes or a large shallow baking dish. Place the endive, one per guest, in baking dish and pour melted butter over them. Sprinkle with salt, pepper and top with dried crumbs. Bake in oven at 350° until tender.

NUTMEAT LOAF

3 tablespoons butter
3 onions, chopped fine
4 tablespoons butter (more)
2 large carrots, grated raw
1 stalk celery, minced
3 tablespoons parsley, minced
1½ cups milk
6 eggs
3 cups ground nuts
2 cups soft bread crumbs
　 Salt and pepper
　 Cooking oil

This delicately flavored loaf can be made of either Brazil nuts, almonds or cashews. Peel and mince the onions and celery and sauté them lightly in butter. Remove them to a bowl and make a white sauce with the milk and flour in the remaining butter in the skillet. You may need to add a bit more butter. Put the carrots, bread crumbs and nut meats through a meat grinder, then add them to onion mixture, parsley and seasonings. Beat the eggs and mix with the white sauce. Now combine the egg sauce with the other ingredients and pour into an oiled loaf pan. Bake for 1 hour at 350°. Serve with a sauce of your choice.

FRUIT FOOL

In England a Fruit Fool is often served at the end of a family meal. It is a simple dessert made with sweetened, pureed fruit, either cooked or fresh depending on the season. A Fruit Fool can be made with any one of a wide variety of fruits such as berries, pineapple, peaches, bananas, papayas, apricots, applesauce, plums, or whatever may be available. Prepare the fruit ahead of time and refrigerate. Just before serving, whip cream in the amount needed to serve the number of guests. Swirl the fruit through the whipped cream and serve in individual shallow dessert dishes. Some like to add a flavoring to the whipped cream, but you may like to try different ones depending on the fruit used. You can puree fruit in a blender easily.

DEVONSHIRE STRAWBERRIES

2 pints fresh strawberries
1½ cups dairy sour cream
¼ cup brown sugar, firmly packed

Wash and hull the strawberries. Place in a large glass bowl. Cover and chill. Measure soft brown sugar by packing it firmly in measuring cup. Combine with sour cream. Beat until well combined. Pour over strawberries and serve. Serves 6.

LEMON CURD

¼ cup unsalted butter
½ cup granulated sugar (extra fine)
½ cup sugar cubes
2 lemons, juice of
Grated rind from 2 lemons
3 eggs

Briefly, 2 or 3 minutes, place lemons in hot water. This makes them easier to squeeze for juice.

Place butter and sugars in the top of a double boiler. If you prefer, you can use 1 cup of extra fine granulated sugar rather than half cubes. Grate the rind from lemons and squeeze for juice. Add juice and grated rind to the butter and sugar in the pan. Beat the eggs, then stir them into the mixture. Cook over the hot water, stirring constantly until the sugar dissolves and the mixture thickens, but *do not allow to boil.*

Pour into clean canning jars and seal. Lemon curd keeps for quite a while refrigerated. It is one of the tastiest of spreads for toast being both sweet and tart, and a favorite all over Great Britain.

CURRANT BUNS

½ pound all-purpose flour
Pinch of salt
½ stick of margarine (2 oz.)
2 tablespoons sugar
1 egg
½ cup lukewarm water
¼ cup currants
½ teaspoon mixed spices or allspice
½ oz. yeast

Rub the margarine into the salted flour. This makes the texture like small crumbs, smaller than you would get by the usual methods of cutting in with pastry cutter.

When well mixed, make a small well in the center and stir in the egg. Add the yeast to the warm water and stir in the sugar. Add this yeast and sugar water to the flour and egg mixture, kneading it well. Pat it into a mound and leave it to rise to double its bulk.

When dough has risen, knead the currants and spice very lightly into the dough on floured board. Shape into buns (about 8) and place them on a greased baking sheet. Allow the buns to rest for 10 minutes. Bake in hot oven (450°F.) for 5 minutes then lower the heat to 350° and cook for another 5 minutes.

While the buns are baking, put a tablespoon of sugar into a little water, just enough to moistened it, then add 1 cup of milk. Boil the sugar and milk hard for 2 to 3 minutes, then cool. While the buns are still hot from the oven, paint them lightly with pastry brush dipped in the sugar-milk glacé.

— SCOTLAND —

OATMEAL MUSHROOM PATTIES

Note: The Scots properly call the uncooked rolled oats 'oatmeal'. When it is cooked, it is porridge, or oatmeal porridge.

2½ cups rolled uncooked oatmeal
    (do not use instant kind)
 1 4-oz. can chopped mushrooms
 3 eggs, beaten
 1 onion, chopped
 1 teaspoon salt
 ¼ teaspoon powdered thyme

  Mix all ingredients and shape into patties. Fry in butter or oil, but do not use margarine. Fry about 5 minutes on each side and serve immediately. Serves 6.

SCOTTISH SHORTBREAD

2 cups all-purpose flour
1 cup butter
½ cup sugar
   (do NOT substitute margarine or oil)

  Cut butter and sugar together and gradually add flour. It will be very stiff, difficult to work and crumbly. When thoroughly mixed, form into a ball and wrap in wax paper and place in the refrigerator for one or two hours. It will be even more crumbly and hard to work when you take it out. Use a small cookie sheet with ¾″ sides or less. Press mixture evenly onto sheet about ¼ an inch thick. Pack it firmly together using a wooden potato masher or the flat end of a wooden rolling pin. Really pound it together firmly, making certain all the edges are firm.

  Next, take a dinner fork and begin in one corner and make diagonal lines to the lower opposite corner. Skipping about an inch or more between, mark with diagonal fork tracks. Then from the opposite angle, do the same thing to make a light plaid design over the entire top of the dough.

  Place in a preheated oven set at 375°F. and immediately turn heat down to 325°F. Bake about 15 minutes, or until top is a very light brown. Do not let brown on top or the bottom will be burned. Remove from oven and let cool for a few minutes before cutting into pieces about 1½ by 2 inches. Let cool before removing them from sheet or it will crumble.

BROWN BETTY
(or, SCALLOPED APPLES)

2 cups sifted fine bread crumbs or cubed stale bread
3 cups green apples, pared and sliced (approx. 4 to 5 apples)
1 cup brown sugar
¼ cup water
¼ teaspoon cinnamon
½ teaspoon nutmet or mace
1 lemon rind, grated
1½ tablespoons lemon juice
2 tablespoons melted butter

In the bottom of a well-buttered baking casserole put ⅓ of the bread. Mix the apple slices, sugar, water, spices, lemon peel and juice; put half of this mixture into the crumb-lined dish. Cover the fruit mixture with half of the remaining crumbs. Next put in the rest of the apple mixture and top with the last of the crumbs. Pour the melted butter over the top and cover. Bake in oven heated to 375°F. for ½ hour. Remove cover and continue baking until the apples are tender and the crumbs are brown — about ½ hour longer. Serve warm with cream. Serves 4.

GREAT BRITAIN

— WALES —

KEDGEREE

4 onions, chopped
4 tablespoons butter (¼ cup)
1 small cooking apple
1 cup (heaping) brown rice
3 cups water
1 cup milk
   Pinch of dry mustard
   Pinch of nutmeg
1¾ cups cheese, grated
   Salt and pepper to taste

Peel and chop onions and sauté in butter until transparent, not brown, about 10 minutes. Add the grated apple to onions. Wash and pick any hard pieces from the rice, then add to onions and pour 3 cups of boiling water over it. Cover and simmer very slowly for 20 minutes, or until rice is tender. Heat the milk and pour it over the rice, then gradually add the grated cheese, mustard and nutmeg. Season with salt and pepper to taste and serve immediately. Serves 4.

WELSH RAREBIT

1 teaspoon dry mustard
1 teaspoon paprika
1 teaspoon salt
1 teaspoon Worcestershire or soy sauce
2 cups sharp cheddar cheese cut up small
½ cup homogenized milk or half milk, half cream

Melt the butter in top of double boiler; add the cut up cheese. Stir to aid melting of the cheese and when melted add the seasonings. Stirring rapidly and constantly, add the milk and stir until smooth. Pour over hot buttered toast triangles and top with slice of tomato. Serve immediately.

LEEK CASSEROLE

2 bunches of fresh leeks
3 tablespoons butter
2 tablespoons flour
1 cup milk
½ cup grated cheese
  Salt, to taste
  Dash of paprika

Make a white sauce of melted butter, milk, and flour, stirring constantly until thickened. Clean leeks. They usually come two to three to a bunch. Cut off root strings at bottom and most of the green tops. Leave them whole and par-boil until just tender. Cut into 1½-inch pieces and place the leeks in a buttered casserole dish and pour white sauce over them and sprinkle with the grated cheese and a dash of paprika on top. Place in broiler under flame until cheese is melted and crisp and brown. For variety, you may include the grated cheese in the sauce and sprinkle top with bread crumbs. Reheat for 15 minutes in 350° oven.

Leeks are the national symbol of Wales, and their delicate oniony flavor adds zest to soups, minces and vegetable dishes of all kinds.

PEACH-MACAROON MOLD

1 dozen 2 inch dry macaroons*
1 can (29 oz.) sliced cling peaches, drained and diced
  Syrup of peach and water to make 1½ cups liquid
1 cup cold water
3 envelopes vegetarian unflavored* or lemon gelatin
1 tablespoon lemon juice
½ teaspoon almond extract
2 cups heavy cream, whipped
2 egg whites
⅛ teaspoon salt
½ cup sugar

1. Gently crush maracroons to make fine crumbs (about 1 cup); set aside.
2. Soften gelatin following envelope instructions with 1 cup cold water in saucepan. Dissolve. Stir in peach syrup and water, lemon juice, and extract.
3. Chill until slightly thickened. Fold in macaroon crumbs, diced peaches, and whipped cream.
4. Beat egg whites and salt until frothy. Gradually add sugar, continuing to beat until peaks are formed. Spread over gelatin mixture and gently fold together until blended. Turn into a 2-quart mold. Chill at least 6 hours. Unmold onto a chilled serving plate. Makes about 12 servings.

* If necessary, dry macaroons on a baking sheet in a 325°F. oven a few minutes. Watch carefully.

Tea

GREECE

Easter Buffet Menu
or
Special Luncheon for Guests

Greek Egg-Lemon Soup
Athenian Green Salad
Moussaka
Spanakopita (Greens Pie)
Rice Stuffed Tomatoes
Red Hardcooked Eggs   Fruit-Vegetable Gelatin
Cantaloupe with Honey   Greek Pastries
Turkish Coffee

EGG-LEMON SOUP

3   egg yolks
½   cup sugar
½   teaspoon lemon rind
1   teaspoon lemon juice
1   teaspoon vanilla
4   cups (1 qt.) buttermilk
½   cup cream, whipped
    Blanched almonds slivered,
    Finely minced mint leaves,
    Fresh raspberries

Beat the egg yolks with an electric mixer and gradually add the sugar. When it forms a ribbon, add the lemon juice, grated lemon rind and vanilla. Very slowly beat in the buttermilk until smooth. Serve in individual bowls which have been chilled. Sprinkle a pinch or two of finely minced mint leaves, slivered almonds and a few fresh raspberries on top, and add a dab of whipped cream.

ATHENIAN GREEN SALAD

3   heads lettuce—1 each of romaine, butter, iceberg—torn into bite size pieces
1   avocado, peeled, sliced
2   tomatoes, peeled, cut into wedges
2   dozen Greek style olives (or pitted ripe olives)
1   small jar (4 oz.) sweet red pimento, drained
¼   pound Feta cheese, crumbled

Wash and dry greens which have become crisp in a cellophane bag placed in refrigerator the day before. Pile and toss greens in a large wooden salad bowl. Pour dressing (recipe follows) and toss gently again. Arrange tomato wedges, avocado slices, olives, pimentos on top and sprinkle Feta cheese over entire top.

DRESSING

Pour into clean jar with tight lid, ¾ cup olive oil, ¼ cup red wine vinegar, ½ teaspoon each of salt and garlic salt, and ⅛ teaspoon freshly ground pepper. Cover jar and shake well. Chill. Pour over Athenian Salad and toss before adding garnish. Makes about 1 cup, plenty for the above salad.

MOUSSAKA

This dish has been the great classic of the Near East. It has been included in the cuisine of almost every country in Asia Minor and the Balkans, plus several in North Africa. There are many variations, naturally, but this vegetarian version is popular simply because it is so good. It travels well for potluck suppers, picnics, and is good served at any temperature.

2 large, unblemished eggplants
4 large onions
2 teaspoons sugar
1 garlic clove, peeled, crushed
1 large can Italian pear-shaped, peeled tomatoes, drain and save juice (1 lb., 12 oz. size)
½ teaspoon crumbled rosemary
2 tablespoons minced parsley
½ teaspoon salt
½ teaspoon pepper
1 can (15 oz.) heavy tomato purée
  Olive oil

Wash eggplant and slice, unpeeled, into ½-inch thick slices; salt and oil on both sides with pastry brush dipped in olive oil. Place on cookie sheet to broil quickly on both sides.
Take two 8 x 10 inch shallow baking dishes that can also be used for serving in, such as pyrex, (or one large one 13 x 9 inches or more). Cover the bottom of the dish with the 4 large onions that have been chopped and sautéed until translucent, then add 2 teaspoons sugar and continue sautéing until golden brown base appears. Add the freshly peeled and crushed garlic clove. Drain the canned tomatoes and save juice. Add tomatoes, rosemary, parsley, salt and pepper to onion mixture. Next add the purée and stir in well. Simmer uncovered, stirring occasionally, for a half hour. Spoon half this sauce into the bottoms of the two baking dishes, then add the previously broiled slices of eggplant. Layer with more sauce and reserved tomato juice, then spread with the folowing cheese filling and top with more tomato sauce.

CHEESE FILLING:

2 lbs. pot cheese
1 cup freshly grated Parmesan cheese
⅛ teaspoon mace
⅛ teaspoon rosemary, crumbled
⅛ teaspoon pepper
½ teaspoon salt
2 large eggs

Blend all ingredients and generously spread filling over eggplant in baking dish. Repeat until all layers are finished, ending with the rest of the Parmesan all over top. Bake in oven heated to 375° for 45 minutes, uncovered. Allow to stand 15 minutes before serving. This dish can be refrigerated, covered, for several hours before baking.

SPANAKOPITA (Greens Pie)

These are pastry squares filled with Feta cheese and assorted greens, and are delicious either warm or chilled. If there is a Greek market near you, you may be able to buy the tissue-thin sheets of dough, called "fila", in 1-pound packages. If not, frozen pastry shells can be bought, defrosted, rolled and cut for use. Or, if you are an expert cook, you can use a flaky pastry recipe, rolled especially thin and cut into squares.

FILLING:

1 bunch Swiss chard
1 bunch spinach
1 chicory or curly endive
  Parsley
  Green onions
½ cup butter
¼ cup olive oil
1 teaspoon salt
½ teaspoon pepper
4 beaten eggs
¾ lb. Feta cheese, crumbled
10 fila (approx. 12 x 16 inches) pastry sheets

Wash the greens well, drain and chop fine. Pat dry with paper towels. Mix the remaining ingredients into the greens thoroughly.

Lay out 10 sheets of fila and cover with plastic to keep from drying out. Melt ½ cup butter, and with a pastry brush, lightly butter five of the sheets of pastry, one at a time, and lay one on top of the other in a buttered 9 x 13 baking pan. (If using flaky pastry, you won't need to stack but about two thin rolled sheets.) Place the greens mixture on top of buttered fila and sprinkle lightly with cinnamon. Fold any fila hanging over the sides back over the top of greens. Arrange 5 more buttered sheets of fila, this time cutting to fit the pan. With a sharp paring knife, cut small squares through the top layers of pastry. Bake in 400° oven for 1 hour, or until greens are tender. Cover top with foil, remove to rack to cool and cut into squares. Serve hot or cold.

RICE-STUFFED TOMATOES

8 large firm tomatoes
2 teaspoons salt
½ teaspoon black pepper
¾ cup olive oil
1 cup chopped white onion
½ cup raw rice (not the 'instant' variety)
2 tablespoons currants or seedless raisins
1 cup boiling water
2 tablespoons minced fresh parsley
¼ cup pine nuts or blanched almonds
½ cup dry bread crumbs

Cut ½-inch pieces off the stem-end of tomatoes; reserve tops. Scoop out the pulp without breaking the skin. With half the salt and pepper, sprinkle the inside of tomato shells. Chop the tomato pulp. Heat ½ cup of oil in saucepan and brown the chopped onions. Stir in the raw rice until all coated. Add the tomato pulp, currants and remaining salt and pepper. Add water and cover. Cook 10 minutes over low heat. Mix in parsley and minced nuts. Taste for seasoning, add what is needed. Stuff the tomatoes loosely with the mixture, then sit the tops on them. In an oiled baking dish, arrange the stuffed tomatoes and brush them with the remaining oil. Sprinkle with bread crumbs and bake in 350° oven for 45 minutes. Can be served hot or cold, in Greece they are usually cold.

RED HARDCOOKED EGGS

If these are prepared ahead of time, of course, red food coloring or Easter egg dye may be used and they are dyed in the shell. Another way they are prepared is to peel and chill the hardboiled eggs, then soak them in the juice from pickled beets which adds only a bit of flavor to them and soaks through the egg white only a bit, leaving the yolks untouched. Red eggs are an Easter tradition for the children.

FRUIT AND VEGETABLE GELATIN

2 pkgs. (3 oz. each) vegetarian lemon gelatin
  Water
1 small jar sliced pimentos
  Stuffed green olives
½ cup canned mandarin oranges
1 cup crisp cooked baby lima beans
8 thin slices of firm tomato or cucumber

Following the directions on the package of gelatin, keep in mind that vegetarian gelatin jells much more quickly than the animal-rennet variety does. Divide the gelatin in half quickly, keeping half soft in the top part of a double boiler over hot, not boiling, water.

In your gelatin mold, have ready olives and pimento slices arranged in bottom. Add the ½ cup canned mandarin slices to the first half of gelatin and pour into mold over the olives and pimentos. Arrange the thin slices of tomato or cucumber on top and let chill to firm.

Into the second half of gelatin in the double boiler, fold 1 cup of baby lima beans and when first half is firm, pour this mixture over it. Chill overnight. When ready to serve garnish each serving with melon balls and freshly rinsed mint leaves.

In Greek market or bakery, you can purchase a lovely selection of traditional Greek breads and pastries. Kouloura is the doughnut-shaped bread which goes so well with this meal. In pastries you will want to try Koulourakia (Easter shortbread), Kourabiedes (Sugar-coated butter cakes), and Amigthalopeta (Almond cake). And finish off your dinner with strong, Turkish coffee-Ibrik!

CANTALOUPE WITH HONEY

Seed and peel the melon; cut into bite-size pieces and chill. Blend 1 tablespoon honey with juice from 1 lemon. Stir this into ½ cup whipping cream and whip until softly thickened. Serve over the melon cubes in glass, footed sherbet compotes.

HAWAII

Dinner Menu
Hard Cooked Eggs with
Caper Sauce
Fried Avocado
Savoury Rice
Spinach Salad
Ambrosia
Demi Tasse Served on Patio
or in the Garden

HARDCOOKED EGGS WITH CAPER SAUCE

6 to 8 hardcooked eggs, cooled and peeled
1 cup mayonnaise
4 tablespoons drained capers
4 tablespoons minced parsley
2 teaspoons of liquid from capers jar
Paprika

Cut the hardcooked eggs in half and arrange on serving dish. Combine all the other ingredients to make the sauce; makes about 1½ cups of sauce. Pour over eggs and sprinkle top with paprika.

FRIED AVOCADO

1 large or 2 medium avocados
1 egg, beaten
Salt
1 cup crack crumbs
Butter for frying

Peel avocado and slice around, not lengthwise, to remove the seed. Then proceed to slice in ⅛ inch rings. Lightly beat the egg in a shallow dish and add salt. Dip each avocado in beaten egg, then into cracker crumbs and fry quickly in butter, pouring the remainder of the beaten egg into the center of the rings. Turn carefully with a pancake turner. Serve with Savoury Rice. This also makes an excellent main dish.

SAVOURY RICE

1 cup brown or white rice
1 cup canned tomatoes
2 onions, chopped
1 green pepper, seeded and chopped
½ lb. mushrooms, chopped
Olive oil for sautéing
4 oz. cashew nuts milled
2 eggs, hardcooked and chopped
Juice and grated rind of ½ lemon
2 or 3 bay leaves
2 tablespoons parsley, minced
1/16 teaspoon ground cloves
Salt and freshly ground pepper
Grated Swiss Cheese

Boil rice and hard cook the eggs. Sauté onions and green pepper in olive oil or butter until lightly brown. Add drained tomatoes and mushrooms with seasonings. Simmer for about 20 minutes. Remove bay leaves.

To the rice add the cashews which have been milled in a regular meat grinder, chopped eggs, parsley and lemon juice and grated rind. Season carefully with salt and pepper. Mix thoroughly and place entire mixture in a buttered casserole dish and bake for 20 minutes at 325°. Grated cheese may be sprinkled over top before baking if you like. Serves 4.

SPINACH SALAD

6 to 8 beets, cooked or canned, drained and sliced
1 large package (1 pound) fresh spinach
2 garlic cloves, crushed
1 medium red onion, in rings
   Juice of ½ lemon
6 radishes, optional
3 tablespoons cider vinegar
6 tablespoons salad oil
12 seedless ripe olives
   Green Goddess Salad Dressing

Marinate the beets with garlic, salt, pepper, vinegar and 4 tablespoons salad oil. Mix together the lemon juice, salt and pepper and pour over the spinach which has been torn into bite size. Place spinach in a mound in the middle of a round plate. To serve, make a ring of marinated beet slices around the spinach and place a few on top. Sprinkle beets with minced chives or parsley. If you do not like garlic flavor you may flavor the marinade with orange or lemon rind instead.

Although spinach must be rinsed a number of times because of the fine sand which clings to the curly leaves, and though it must also be deveined, it makes the tastiest of salads. Also, spinach is the only green salad which stays crisp as a leftover and can be served at the next meal.

After cleaning and veining the spinach, break into bite size pieces. Slice the red onion into very thin rings and arrange on top of spinach and beets. Cut ripe olives in halves and do the same.

For variety, small crunchy flowerettes from cauliflower and sliced hardcooked eggs can be added to this salad, if served as a main dish. Serves 4 to 6.

AMBROSIA

This simple and tasty dessert can be prepared quickly. It only has two ingredients— oranges and shredded coconut. Peel and section the oranges over the bowl so as to catch all juices. Peel the white skins from the sections or, if necessary, use a sharp paring knife. Sprinkle with sweetened coconut and mix together thoroughly. Let chill for half an hour before serving either in a large bowl for guests to help themselves, or in individual serving compotes. You adjust the number of oranges and the amount made to the number of guests.

Luncheon Menu
Island Pot Pie
Peas and Rice Aloha
Pineapple Salad with
Curry Dressing
Baked Hawaiian Papaya
Orange Sherbert
or
King Kamehameha Pie
Lemon-balm Iced Tea

ISLAND POT PIE

2 eggs, slightly beaten
1 cup cracker crumbs
1 can "choplets" (20-oz. can)*
6 hardcooked eggs
1 small onion
2 stalks of celery, chopped
1 package oven-ready biscuits, unbaked
Egg Gravy

Dip choplets in beaten egg and then into cracker crumbs. Sauté in salad oil or peanut oil. Place in flat baking dish. On top scatter the chopped celery, chopped onion and 3 hard-boiled eggs sliced, and pour gravy from can (to which the other three eggs have been chopped and added) covering it. Then top with biscuits and bake in 425° oven until biscuits are done and golden brown. Serves 5

*Juicy vegetarian protein fillets made from wheat protein. Each fillet is packed in a savory broth flavored with mushrooms, vegetables and yeast extract. Sold in health food stores. One brand is made by Worthington Foods.

PEAS AND RICE ALOHA

2 cups rice
1 clove garlic
1 green pepper, seeded and chopped
1 cup June green peas, cooked
2 cups canned tomatoes, in small pieces
Olive oil
Sweet red pepper or small jar of pimento

Wash rice and cook in four cups of boiling water with a peeled clove of garlic. While rice is cooking, combine chopped green pepper, canned tomatoes with the juice from the can and a small amount of olive oil. When water has evaporated from the rice add the sauce made from all the other ingredients. Simmer rice in this sauce for 15 minutes. When almost ready to serve, add the green peas. Line a dinner plate with new green spinach leaves and chop up a few to make a nest in the center. Pour rice into nest and top with tiny strips of pimento or sweet red pepper and serve immediately.

PINEAPPLE SALAD

1 3-oz. package cream cheese
2 small cans pineapple slices
8 oz. macadamia nuts
   Lettuce

Crush all but a few of the macadamia nuts, not too fine. Soften the cream cheese then add a few spoons of the juice from canned pineapple to soften a bit more. Stir in the crushed nut meats. Arrange lettuce on salad plates and 2 slices of pineapple on each. Roll a heaping tablespoon of the cheese mixture and place it in the center hole of each pineapple slice. Sprinkle a few whole nuts around each plate and top with Curry Dressing.

CURRY DRESSING FOR SALAD

¼ cup dairy sour cream
¼ cup mayonnaise
¼ teaspoon Madras*curry powder
1 tablespoon lemon juice
⅛ teaspoon dry mustard
   Pinch of garlic salt

Sprinkle curry powder into mixture of mayonnaise and sour cream. Add lemon juice, dry mustard and garlic salt. Mix thoroughly and chill for at least an hour. Before serving, taste and add more curry powder if you wish.

*East Indian curry sold in square tins in large food markets.

BAKED HAWAIIAN PAPAYA

2 Hawaiian Papayas
4 tablespoons brown sugar
4 teaspoons butter
   Cinnamon
   Nutmeg
   Lemon or Lime wedges

Cut each papaya in half lengthwise. With spoon, scoop out seeds and discard. Sprinkle each half with cinnamon, nutmeg and some brown sugar. Place a teaspoon butter in the hollow of each papaya half and place them cut side up in baking pan or cookie sheet. Bake at 300° for 30 minutes. Serve with lemon or lime wedge. Makes 4 servings.

ORANGE SHERBET

¾ cup orange juice
1½ cups granulated sugar
3 cups cold water
   Grated rind of 1 orange

Soak grated orange rind in the orange juice. Boil sugar and water for 20 minutes to make a syrup; allow to cool and add the orange juice, the rind and pour into ice or freezer tray to freeze. When it begins to freeze, stir it up thoroughly. Then, when it has frozen, stir and mash with large spoon and return to freezer again. Follow these directions and you will have a smooth sherbet without flakes. Makes 1 quart.

KING KAMEHAMEHA PIE

- 1   12-oz. can pineapple juice
- ¾   cup sugar
- 7   cooking apples, peeled, cored and cut in wedges (about 7 cups)
- 3   tablespoons cornstarch
- 1   tablespoon butter
- 1   teaspoon pure vanilla extract
- ¼   teaspoon salt
- 1   baked 9-in. pastry shell, cooled
    Whipping cream
- 2   teaspoons sugar
    Macadamia Nuts

In a large saucepan combine 1½ cups of pineapple juice and ¾ cup of sugar. Bring to boiling point and add apples. Simmer, covered, until tender but not soft — 3 to 4 minutes. Lift apples from syrup and set aside to drain. Combine cornstarch and remaining pineapple juice, then add it to the syrup in saucepan. Cook and stir until thick and bubbly, then continue for another minute. Remove from heat and add butter, vanilla and salt. Cool for 10 minutes without stirring. Pour half of the syrup into baked pastry shell, spread to completely cover the bottom. Arrange the apples on top of syrup. Spoon the remaining syrup over apples, cover and chill. Whip the heavy cream, add 2 teaspoons sugar and 1 teaspoon vanilla. Beat to stiff peaks. Serve topped with whipped cream and macadamia nuts.

LEMON-BALM ICED TEA

- 12   leaves of lemon balm
- 2   teaspoons sugar
    Juice of ½ lemon
- 1   whole clove
- 4   tablespoons green tea or English Breakfast tea
- 5   cups boiling water

Crush the lemon balm leaves with the sugar, lemon juice and clove to make a thoroughly blended green paste. Add the tea leaves and pour the boiling water over tea and paste. Sir, cover, cool and refrigerate. To serve strain the mixture and serve with a bowl of ice, a small dish of lemon balm leaves and a jar of honey. Each guest may flavor and sweeten to taste. Makes about 6 cups.

HUNGARY

Dinner For A Winter Evening
Bab Leves (Speckled Bean Soup)
Oriental Patties
Tomato and Cottage Cheese Salad
Fruit Rice Pudding

BAB LEVES
Speckled Bean Soup
(An Old Hungarian Recipe)

1   lb. dried pinto or cranberry beans
2   carrots
1   parsnip
1   large onion, peeled and halved
1   clove garlic, peeled
5   sprigs parsley
1   teaspoon salt
2   tablespoons butter
2   tablespoons flour
2   teaspoons Hungarian paprika
    Sour cream

Cover beans with cold water and soak overnight.

Peel and prepare the carrots, parsnip, onion and garlic. Leave garlic clove whole and do not press or crush. Drain the beans which have soaked overnight but reserve the water. Measure the bean water and add enough additional water to make 3 quarts total. Put water and beans in a large soup kettle—large enough to hold at least 6 quarts. Add carrots, parsnip, onion halves, garlic and parsley to pot and simmer, covered, for about two hours. Pour through strainer or colander, returning beans and broth to kettle but reserving the carrots and parsnip whole. Simmer, again covered, until beans are tender (about 1 hour). Slice carrots and parsnip and add to soup with 1 teaspoon salt.

Melt two tablespoons butter in a small saucepan, add 2 tablespoons flour and 2 teaspoons sweet Hungarian paprika, stirring constantly for about 5 minutes. When this roux is made, ladle out about 1 cup of the soup broth and gradually mix with roux to thin it, then return all of it to the soup kettle. Cook about 5 minutes more to let the soup thicken slightly, then serve steaming bowls of this delicious bean soup with a dollop of sour cream in each bowl. Serve thick, crusty bread with it.

"ORIENTAL" PATTIES

4 eggs, beaten
1 cup vegetarian burger (canned)*
¾ cup quick rolled oats
1 green pepper, finely chopped
¼ cup milk
½ cup chopped onion
1 teaspoon salt
1 tablespoon soy sauce

Combine all ingredients and mix thoroughly. Form into flat patties and sauté in oil over low heat. Brown on both sides. Serve with additional soy sauce as condiment. Makes 6 to 8 patties. Serves 4. To complete your meal with an Oriental theme, serve rice with butter and soy sauce, green vegetable salad and a dessert such as Peaches with an Almond Cookie.

*Mildly seasoned vegetarian protein burger. Can be used in roasts, patties, burgers and chili. Sold in speciality markets or health food stores.

TOMATO AND COTTAGE CHEESE SALAD

Make individual servings in salad bowls or on salad plates lined with crisp lettuce leaves. Place two or three slices or quarters of firm, ripe tomato on the lettuce bed and mound a scoop of cottage cheese on top. Sprinkle lightly with paprika and serve with homemade mayonnaise. (See France for Mayonnaise recipe.)

FRUIT RICE PUDDING

2 cups white rice
4 cups milk
6 tablespoons butter
10 tablespoons brown sugar
2 eggs, separated
1 lemon rind, grated
3 to 4 tablespoons seeded raisins
Sliced fresh apples or peaches

Cook 2 cups of rice in 4 cups of milk until milk is all absorbed and rice is soft. If the rice is not tender, add more milk and continue cooking. Cool.

Mix 6 tablespoons of butter with 10 tablespoons of brown sugar; when well creamed, add the yolks of 2 eggs and the grated lemon rind.

Mix the cold rice with the egg yolk mixture and add a handful of seeded raisins.

Beat the egg whites until stiff and dry. Gently fold the beaten whites into the rice mixture. Butter a baking dish and sprinkle with fine, dry bread crumbs, removing the excess crumbs which do not stick.

Put a layer of the rice mixture on the bottom of dish, then a generous layer of sliced fruit, then a layer of rice, then fruit, etc.

This pudding is very popular in Hungarian homes. It can be served hot or cold but my friends eat it hot.

Bake in a moderate oven, 350°, until brown. Serves 8.

INDIA

Favorite Indian Foods

Indian Curry Chutney
Condiment Tray of Chopped Dishes
Fried Coconut   Baked Bananas
Bhonee Khichri   Schillo
Dahl   Pulao
Bombay Eggs with Almond-Raisin Rice
Halva   Hot Tea

INDIAN CURRY CHUTNEY

1 small apple
2 tablespoons chopped onion
2 tablespoons butter, more if necessary
⅛ teaspoon powdered clove
1 teaspoon lemon juice
1 tablespoon curry powder

Peel and cut apple and onion and sauté in pan with 1 tablespoon butter; allow to brown lightly. Then squash into a paste and add curry powder, clove and lemon juice. Simmer slowly for 10 minutes. This basic curry mixture is now ready. It can be mixed with water from the cooked rice, stirred put into the cream sauce over an egg- or vegetable curry, over the rice to be served, or any number of ways.

To make a vegetable curry add 3 cups of chopped, raw vegetables to the above basic curry with a very little water, lightly salted, the amount should be no more than would barely cover the vegetables in a pan. Cover the pan and let simmer slowly until the water is absorbed and the vegetable is crisply done.

Vegetables which lend themselves to curry are cauliflower, fresh peas, baby lima beans, fresh string beans, celery, young carrots and summer squash.

Besides a wide array of chopped condiments, sautéed coconut and sautéed or baked bananas are accompaniments to curry. Serve rice and Indian chutney with curries.

CONDIMENT TRAY

Chopped hard cooked eggs, put through a potato ricer, or chopped very fine, are nearly always served as one of the condiments for curry dishes. Others, all chopped very fine and arranged in small separate dishes or sections of tray, would include pineapple, cashews, red onion, chives, raisins, coconut shredded fine and chopped, firm green tomatoes, ripe yellow and red tomatoes without their seeds, celery, banana, apple and avocado (these last three should be sprinkled with lemon juice to prevent turning), cucumber and any fresh or canned and drained fruits you might like to add for color and taste variety. These are passed and sprinkled over the top of the hot curried dishes.

FRIED COCONUT

Coconuts grow in tropical climates and provide meat and drink for what is estimated to be around 300 million people in various countries. Coconuts are used by these masses of the world's population in some form every day.

To open a coconut, find one of the soft spots at the top of the shell. You can take an ice pick or a similar sharp, strong instrument and pierce these spots and drain the milk from it. Then tap all over the shell with a hammer until the hard shell cracks and literally falls off. Natives throw gently but firmly on a rock or cement.

You can also break the shell by heating an oven to 350°F. and placing the coconut in the oven for 30 minutes.

Now that you have freed the fresh coconut meat from the shell, cut it in small strips with a peeler or sharp knife. Fry the strips in butter until golden brown, drain on paper towels and serve.

BAKED BANANAS

Bananas (number depends on number of persons to be served; allow 6 bananas for 8 persons.) Chose firm ones.

Butter, at least 6 tablespoons
Flour
2 or 3 eggs, well beaten
¾ cup bread crumbs
Salt and pepper, dash
Few drops of lemon juice

Peel bananas, cut in middle and then cut again lengthwise, making four pieces from each banana. Dip each piece in flour, then in the beaten eggs. Place in a well-buttered, shallow baking dish. Sprinkle each with crumbs, a dash of salt and pepper, and a drop or two of lemon juice. Dribble the melted butter over them and bake in hot oven (450°F.) for 15 minutes.

BHONEE KHICHRI

1 cup rice
1 cup lentils, cooked
2 onions, sliced
4 tablespoons butter
  Salt
  Few slices fresh ginger or
½ teaspoon ground ginger
¼ teaspoon ground cloves
1 or 2 bay leaves
1 teaspoon cinnamon

The lentils should be soaked overnight and cooked separately before starting this recipe.

Melt butter and sauté onions to golden brown. Remove onions and set aside. Put rice and cooked and drained lentils into the butter and cook until butter is absorbed. Add ginger and other seasonings. Cover with boiling water and simmer slowly with lid on until water is absorbed and vegetables are done. Serve with fried onions.

SCHILLO (Indian Rice)

1 pound rice, not the "instant" kind
2 quarts cold water
1 stalk celery with leaves, cut fine
6 large leeks (clear green with white bulbs)
¼ teaspoon powdered cloves
6 to 8 bay leaves
1 tablespoon good, imported curry powder
2 teaspoons salt (or to taste)
4 tablespoons olive oil
2 heaping tablespoons minced parsley

Cut or chop all vegetables into small pieces and soak all ingredients, including rice, in the two quarts of water. Soak in the big pot they are to be cooked in for 3 to 4 hours. After soaking, boil over very slow flame, simmer for 1½ hours. Turn over occasionally to prevent rice from sticking. Add a little boiling water, if necessary. This makes a very delicious, unusual and inexpensive dish.

DAHL

2 or 3 onions, chopped
1 large clove of garlic, peeled, chopped
¼ teaspoon thyme
  Salt to taste
1 teaspoon curry powder or more, to taste
1½ cups green split peas
2 tomatoes
1 green pepper
  Butter

In butter, sauté chopped onion, garlic, thyme, dash of ground ginger, and curry powder. Follow directions on package for soaking split green peas overnight. Drain the soaked peas but reserve the water, and add to the onion mixture and simmer gently for a few minutes. Add the reserved water, chopped tomatoes and chopped green pepper and salt, and simmer till the peas are done. Serve over rice. This may be served as a separate course or eaten with curry.

PULAO

1 cup rice
2 onions, peeled and sliced
2 tablespoons raisins
2 tablespoons almonds, sliced
½ teaspoon cinnamon
  Few cardamon seeds
1 or 2 bay leaves
¾ cup butter
  Saffron
½ teaspoon salt

Put 4 tablespoons butter in a saucepan and add the sliced onions, sauté until brown. Add the rice and the remainder of the butter and cook until the rice has absorbed most of the butter, stirring all the time. Add the other ingredients and just cover with boiling water. Put cover on saucepan and simmer slowly. When done, it should be put in the oven for about 10 minutes before serving. Sprinkle top with saffron and serve.

BOMBAY EGGS WITH ALMOND-RAISIN RICE

1 cup whole blanched almonds
½ cup milk
1½ cups raisins
½ cup water
1 tablespoon curry powder
½ teaspoon salt
  Dash of white pepper
  Shredded coconut, preferably fresh unsweetened
  Sliced green onions with tops
½ teaspoon powdered sugar

2 tablespoons butter
2½ cups hot steamed rice
3 tablespoons each butter and flour
1 cup milk
½ teaspoon salt
12 hardcooked eggs
  Watermelon rind pickles
  Mango chutney

Soak almonds in milk for 5 hours to soften them and to give milk some of the almond flavor. Drain well. Later, use the milk as part of the liquid for the curry sauce. Soak raisins in water for 30 minutes; drain. Before serving time, mix the drained almonds with the raisins; sauté over medium heat in the 2 tablespoons of butter for about five minutes. Set aside ½ cup of the mixture to serve as a condiment. Pour remainder over top of hot rice.

Melt the 3 tablespoons butter; stir in equal amounts of flour and add curry powder to make a smooth paste. Gradually add the 1 cup milk drained from soaking the almonds. Cook, stirring constantly, until a smooth sauce has thickened. Add powdered sugar, salt and pepper. Leave hardcooked eggs whole (or you can halve them) and pour sauce over them. Serve immediately. If you must delay, place them in oven at 350°F. to stay warm. Serve two eggs per person if this is to be the main dish for protein. Serve with the almond-raisin topped rice and condiments. Makes 6 servings.

HALVA

- 1 cup brown sugar
- 3 cups water
- ½ cup blanched almonds or pignola (pine nuts), chopped
- ½ cup raisins
- 1 cup butter
- 1 cup cream of wheat or farina

Halva is the best-known of Indian sweets and is not difficult to make. Boil water and brown sugar, and continue cooking a few more minutes to thicken. Add raisins and nuts to this syrup. Take another sauce pan and melt the butter, stirring constantly and add the cream of wheat until the mixture is golden brown. Pour in the already prepared brown sugar syrup and stir constantly until the mixture sticks together in one mass and leaves the sides of the pan. Immediately remove from the heat. Cool before serving. This can be prepared days before serving as it keeps well, by wrapping well in tight container and keeping in the refrigerator.

If you start out with a curry and end with halva you will have had a real Indian meal.

In the Oriental countries everything is placed on the table at once, and everyone helps himself. Therefore in this selection of recipes, there are no courses as the western world serves them. Also you have doubtless noticed that there is more than one rice dish. This, too, is customary since any dish left over from one meal is simply served again at the next, even if it is a breakfast meal.

INDONESIA

Indonesian Dinner

Meatless Indonesian Chicken Salad
with Curry Dressing
Bambu Ratjang (Peanut Sauce)
Gado Gado
Nasi Goreng (Rice Dish)
Soto Jam
Cherry Velvet Cream Dessert
Tea

MEATLESS INDONESIAN CHICKEN SALAD

2 cups diced vegetarian chicken substitute (19 oz. can)
4 fresh pears
½ cup coarsely chopped macadamia nuts
½ cup thinly sliced cucumbers
2 tablespoons thinly sliced green onions
2 tablespoons crystallized ginger slivers
Curry dressing
Lettuce cups
Lemon juice
2 tablespoons flaked coconut

In a big bowl place bite size pieces of vegetarian chicken. Pare, halve, core, and slice 1 pear into bite size pieces. Add to chicken along with nuts, the cucumbers, ginger and onions. Add curry dressing and mix carefully, (recipe follows). The remaining 3 pears are peeled, cored, and halved, dipped in lemon juice and arranged on lettuce cups on individual plates.

Spoon salad onto pear halves, sprinkle with coconut.

Curry dressing and other salad ingredients should be prepared about 30 minutes before serving for flavor to develop.

CURRY DRESSING

1 cup real mayonnaise (no substitute)
4 tablespoons dairy sour cream
1 teaspoon Madras curry powder
1 teaspoon mustard
½ teaspoon allspice
½ teaspoon garlic salt

Mix, and stir well.

GADO GADO

The salad most popular in Indonesia is called Gado Gado. It is made in layers of cooked and raw vegetables topped with some of the "Bambu Ratjang" (peanut sauce).

2 quarts water, salted with
1½ teaspoons salt
1 cup bean sprouts, stringy ends removed
½ medium-sized head of cabbage, leaves cut in 2-inch squares
1½ cups green beans in 1½-inch pieces (or one 9-oz. package frozen cut green beans)
1 large potato, cooked, peeled, diced
2 cucumbers, peeled and in thin halved slices

¾ cup peanut sauce (recipe follows)
1 bunch cleaned, trimmed, thinly sliced radishes which are used as a garnish on top of salad
2 hard cooked eggs in ¼-inch slices

In large kettle, bring the salted water to boil; add bean sprouts and cook just until tender crisp, about 3 minutes; remove with strainer or slotted spoon and drain. Chill in refrigerator.

In same water cook the cabbage until tender (about four minutes), remove from water, drain and refrigerate. Cook green beans in same water just until tender (8 to 10 minutes); remove, drain, reserve vegetable stock for the soup. Allow vegetables to cool.

Layer vegetables on the platter in this order: cabbage, diced potatoes, cucumbers, green beans, and bean sprouts. Sprinkle top of salad with radishes. Pour peanut sauce over the entire salad. Arrange hardcooked egg slices over top. Refrigerate a few minutes before serving.

BAMBU RATJANG
(Peanut Sauce)

Salad oil for cooking
½ medium onion, minced
1 clove garlic, peeled and pressed
1 12-oz. jar chunky-style peanut butter
1 cup coconut milk (Use the commercially frozen variety or make, recipe follows)
2 tablespoons dark brown sugar
1 teaspoon salt
3 dried hot red chilies, seeds removed

Finely mince ½ medium-size onion; fry in ½ inch of hot salad oil in a frying pan until very brown and crisp. Pour off excess oil and remove onions to a mortar (or round bottomed bowl) and mash together with 1 clove of garlic,

pressed to make a smooth paste; return to same frying pan along with 1 jar (12 oz.) chunky-style peanut butter, 1 cup coconut milk (use commercially frozen or make as directed below), 2 tablespoons dark brown sugar, 1 teaspoon salt, and 3 dried hot red chilies (seeds removed) which you have mashed into a paste with a little water. Stir over low heat until smooth, adding water to make it right consistency—like a gravy. Makes about 3 cups sauce.

Coconut Milk

2 cups boiling water, or
2 cups scalded milk
4 cups finely grated fresh coconut, not the pre-packaged sweetened kind

Pour 2 cups boiling water or scalded milk over 4 cups finely grated fresh coconut; let stand 20 minutes. Strain through a double thickness of cheesecloth. Squeeze tightly to remove all liquid. This makes 2 cups.

NASI GORENG

1 cup unpolished rice
5 golden onions chopped fine
1 small red pepper, cut fine
¼ cup soya sauce

Boil 1 cup of rice in salted water. Add the onions finely chopped and 1 or 2 small hot red chilies, cut fine. As these are very hot, add only to taste. Add ¼ cup of soya sauce to onion mixture before simmering. More sauce may be added if needed. This is served with scrambled eggs, tea or coffee.

SOTO JAM
(chicken made of soybean protein and vegetable soup)

    Stock from vegetables or
6 cups water
1 can (20 oz.) meatless "soyameat" chicken
1 teaspoon grated fresh ginger root
1 small clove garlic, minced or pressed
1 can (1 lb.) black-eyed peas, drained
1 medium-sized onion, thinly sliced
2 tablespoons peanut oil
1 tablespoon lemon juice
4 vegetarian bouillon cubes added to vegetable stock or more to taste
1 cup thinly sliced celery
2 hard cooked eggs, in thick slices or chunks

Add to kettle of vegetable stock the vegetarian bouillon cubes, ginger root and garlic. Bring to a boil and cook until ginger root is tender, about 20 minutes. Meanwhile sauté black-eyed peas and onion in ½ inch of oil in a large frying pan for about seven minutes, or until onions are golden, about 7 minutes. Just before serving add cubed chicken (if cooked too long, it will disintegrate) sautéed peas and onions, lemon juice, celery, and egg slices to the stock; heat through. Serve in a large bowl. Serves 4 to 6.

CHERRY VELVET CREAM DESSERT

2 envelopes agar agar plain gelatin
⅛ teaspoon salt
¾ cup sugar
2 cups milk
3 eggs, separated
1 pint sour cream
2 teaspoons vanilla
1 can (1-lb., 4-oz.) cherry pie filling

Follow directions to use the agar agar or other vegetarian gelatin. Combine gelatin, milk, salt and sugar. Place over medium heat, stirring until gelatin dissolves. Beat into the lightly beaten egg yolks. Cool. Stir in the sour cream and vanilla. Whip the egg whites into gelatin mixture. Pour into 7-cup mold and chill until firm.

Unmold onto a serving plate. Spoon the cherry pie filling over the top and garnish with sprigs of mint or sweet woodruff. Makes 8 servings.

IRAN (PERSIA)

Dinner

Melon Compote
Legume et Noix (Vegetable-nut Loaf)
Zucchini Tomato Dish
Rice Pilaf
Middle East Salad and Port Salut
Spicy Rangenak
Demi Tasse

MELON COMPOTE

4   cups melon balls or cubes (use Persian or
    Cranshaw melons, or combine)
1   lime
1   cup water
¾   cup sugar
2   tablespoons chopped, preserved ginger
    Fresh mint

In a bowl, place the melon balls or cubes. Slice the lime into half lengthwise, then slice paper-thin. Mix in with melon. In a small saucepan, simmer water, sugar and ginger until slightly syrup-like or when it will spin a thread when dropped from end of spoon (about 10 minutes). While syrup is still very hot, pour over melon and lime mixture, cover and cool. When cooled, place in refrigerator overnight. Serve in footed sherbet glasses and garnish with a sprig of fresh mint in each glass.

LEGUME ET NOIX
(Vegetable-Nut Loaf)

5   carrots
1   cup walnuts
4   slices quality bread
3   onions, chopped
1   cup celery, diced
1   large, fresh green pepper, diced
1   or 2 eggs
½   teaspoon thyme
4   tablespoons olive oil
    Salt and pepper

Sauté onions, green pepper and celery in olive oil (makes a difference in the flavor—do not substitute other oil). In your food grinder, put carrots, bread and nuts and grind together; add onion mixture and oil in which they were cooked. Blend in the egg and seasonings. Grease loaf pan with cooking oil. Put mixture in loaf pan with cracker crumbs sprinkled on top and dot with butter. Serve with brown gravy. Bake in 350° oven for 45 minutes or until browned. (See Index for Brown Gravy.)

ZUCCHINI TOMATO DISH

- 3 fresh, medium sized zucchini squashes
- 1 large can peeled Italian style tomatoes
- 2 onions, peeled and chopped
- ¼ teaspoon dried basil, crushed
- ¼ teaspoon dried oregano, crushed
- ½ teaspoon fresh or dried parsley
  Olive oil for cooking
  Salt and pepper to taste

In a large skillet pour 2 to 3 tablespoons of olive oil and add the dried herbs while heating. Add the chopped onions and stir while cooking until they become transparent.

Wash the zucchini and remove ends and only peel the portions of the skin which have imperfections or discolorations on them. Slice in rounds very, very thin; add to skillet and cover.

Empty the canned tomatoes into a soup dish and separate into small, bite-sized pieces. Pour juice from can into skillet with zucchini, turning heat down to a slow boil. Although you should keep covered, this should be stirred often in order to make sure all the zucchini rounds are separated and will cook evenly. If the tomato juice cooks out, add a bit of water to keep moist. When zucchini is almost done, add the tomato pieces and continue cooking until done. Add salt and pepper for taste and serve hot with Parmesan cheese for each guest to sprinkle on top if they choose.

RICE PILAF

- 3¾ cups water
- 1 teaspoon salt
- 1 teaspoon oil
- 1½ cups long grain rice
- ½ cup golden raisins
- ½ cup butter

Bring water to boil in large saucepan. Add salt, oil and rice; cover and simmer 25 minutes, or until barely tender. Remove from heat. Mix in the raisins and stir with fork. Heat butter until it bubbles and starts to brown; pour over rice and stir with fork. Cover for 10 minutes. Serves 6 to 8. (Recipe can be doubled so that second helpings can be served.)

MIDDLE EASTERN VEGETABLE SALAD

- 1 small escarole lettuce, washed, shredded and tossed
- 12 raw young spinach leaves
- 1 green pepper, seeded and sliced thin
- 2 cucumbers, peeled and quartered
- 6 plum tomatoes, peeled and quartered
- 1 or 2 sweet thinly chopped red Spanish onions
- 1 threaded, cleaned and chopped stalk of celery
- 6 thinly sliced radishes
- ½ cup finely minced parsley
- 1 tablespoon fresh dill or chervil, chopped finely
- 2½ tablespoons olive oil
- 1 clove garlic peeled and pressed
  Salt and pepper

Toss and serve in a big salad bowl with herbs. Pour the dressing just before serving and toss.

Add other ingredients to salad if you like, such as fresh raw mushrooms thinly sliced, or zucchini. Substitute scallions for the Spanish onions, or use mint in place of chervil or dill.

Fresh herbs are often served as hors-d'oeuvres in Iran. Persian women eat them at the end of the meal with bread and cheese.

Serve with Port Salut or other type of cheese of your preference.

This salad can be prepared early in the day, keeping undressed vegetables separate and covered in refrigerator. Serves 4 to 6.

SPICY RANGENAK

¾ cup coarsely chopped walnuts
1 pound pitted dates
1 teaspoon cinnamon
1½ cups unsifted flour
½ cup buckwheat flour
¾ cup granulated sugar
¼ cup powdered sugar
¾ cup hot melted butter
2 teaspoons cinnamon
2 teaspoons nutmeg
1½ teaspoons cardamom
¾ teaspoon ground cloves

Dust the bottom and sides of a buttered 9" x 13" baking pan with 1 teaspoon cinnamon. Lightly toast ¾ cup coarsely chopped walnuts in moderate oven (350°F.) for 6 to 8 minutes. Mix nuts with 1 pound pitted dates and grind mixture in food grinder, using the coarsest setting. Press date mixture evenly into bottom of pan.

In a heavy frying pan, stir together 1½ cups unsifted all-purpose flour and ½ cup buckwheat flour. Stir flours constantly over moderate heat until lightly browned. Blend in ¾ cup hot melted butter. Reduce heat to low and stir for 10 or 12 minutes until butter collects on surface when you pat mixture in bottom of pan. Mix the 2 teaspoons of cinnamon, nutmeg, cardamon and cloves together and put about half in each of the two containers of sugar, one granulated and powdered. Stir ½ of the spiced granulated sugar into buttered mixture, reserve the other ½ for topping over the flour and butter in pan. Cook for 8 to 10 minutes to a fudgelike consistency, stirring constantly. Cool for 30 minutes. Sift the remainder of the spiced powdered sugar over the top, cut into 1 inch squares. Carefully remove from pan when cool.

IRELAND

Family Dinner Menu
Potato Loaf
Creamed Spinach
Cucumber Salad in Dill
Fresh Berries with Sweet Country Cheese
Irish Soda Bread
Sweet Butter
Irish Tea

POTATO LOAF

This should be prepared a day ahead of serving.

3 tablespoons butter
3 tablespoons flour
1 cup milk
5 or 6 medium-sized potatoes
3 eggs, separated
½ to 1 cup grated natural Swiss Cheese (not processed cheese)
½ teaspoon salt
¼ teaspoon white pepper
1 tablespoon finely chopped fresh parsley

Boil 5 or 6 peeled potatoes and cool. Keep aside.

Take 3 tablespoons butter, melted in sauce pan, and add the 3 tablespoons of flour. Stir in 1 cup of milk, and add salt and pepper. Cook into a thick white sauce. Mash and add the cooled potatoes into the sauce. There should be enough potatoes to make a stiff mixture. Add beaten egg yolks to potato mixture and blend well. Add 1 tablespoon of chopped fresh parsley. Coat a baking dish or bread pan well with melted butter or cooking oil. Beat egg whites and fold into mixture. Pour mixture into buttered dish. Cover the pan and set aside for several hours, or refrigerate overnight.

Half an hour before you are ready to serve, turn out the potato loaf onto an ovenproof platter or pan and sprinkle generously with grated natural Swiss cheese. Do not use processed cheese! Bake in a moderate oven at 375° F. until thoroughly hot and nicely browned all over. Garnish with minced fresh parsley. Serves 4.

CREAMED SPINACH

2 (9 or 10 oz.) packages frozen chopped spinach
1 can cream of mushroom soup

Following the package directions, cook the chopped spinach in small amount of salted water until tender. Drain completely through a strainer and press all of the liquid from it possible. Open a can of cream of mushroom soup. Do not dilute! Add it to the still warm cooked spinach and stir thoroughly. Heat over low heat until soup is serving temperature. Serves 4.

CUCUMBER SALAD IN DILL

4   cucumbers
1   cup boiling water
¾   cup sour cream
¼   cup lemon juice
3   tablespoons minced fresh dill, or dried dill weed (*not* dill seed)
1½ teaspoons salt
⅛   teaspoon pepper
1   teaspoon sugar

Peel the cucumbers and slice very thin. Pour boiling water over them and let stand for five minutes. Drain and plunge them into ice water. Drain again. Mix together the sour cream, lemon juice, dill and seasonings. Pour mixture over the cucumbers and toss until mixed. Chill for an hour before serving. Serves 6 to 8.

FRESH BERRIES WITH CHEESE

4   cups (2 pints) dairy sour cream
6   egg yolks
1   8-oz. package cream cheese
1   cup sugar
3   or 4 strips of lemon peel

In the top of a double boiler heat 4 cups sour cream, stirring until scalded. Mix the 6 thoroughly beaten egg yolks with the softened cream cheese and 1 cup of sugar. Mix a few spoonsful of the hot sour cream with the egg and cream cheese mixture and then return all to the double boiler. Add lemon peel, which has been thinly pared with a vegetable peeler. Cook over simmering water, stirring frequently, until thickened or about 15 minutes. Remove from heat, cover and let stand over the hot water for 15 minutes or more, then discard the lemon peel.

Line a large wire strainer or colander with 3 or 4 thicknesses of cheesecloth and put over other pan for draining. Pour the cheese mixture into cheesecloth and let stand at room temperature for about 2 hours. Gently draw up the loose edges of the cheesecloth and fasten lightly over drained cheese. Continue draining while it chills overnight. Serve as molded, or you can reshape it with a spatula if you want a more elaborate shape. Arrange fresh and sweet plump strawberries around it. Makes about 3 cups.

IRISH SODA BREAD

This bread, which is like a very large biscuit, evolved in a country where farmhouse cooking was extremely simple. The true Irish bread has no butter, but it tastes better with this addition.

3   cups unbleached flour
1   teaspoon salt
1   teaspoon baking soda
2   tablespoons butter
1   cup buttermilk*

Mix flour, salt and baking soda. Cut in the butter until the mixture looks like cornmeal. Add the buttermilk and stir until the dry ingredients are moistened. Turn out the ball of dough and knead for 1 minute, then pat into a round, rather flat cake about the size of a 9-inch pie pan. Place the dough on a buttered cookie sheet and cut a large cross in the top. Bake in oven preheated to 425°F. for about 40 minutes. If the loaf is done, it will sound hollow when you tap it.

* If you have no buttermilk or sour milk on hand you can add 1 tablespoon vinegar to sweet milk and let it stand for 5 minutes before adding to the recipe. This is a handy substitute for any recipe calling for buttermilk.

ISRAEL

Dinner Menu
Falafel with Sauce
Latkes (Potato Pancakes)
Jerusalem Salad
Beets with Horseradish
Blueberry and Apple Blintzes

FALAFEL

1 pound dried chick peas
3 slices of bread
2 hot peppers
3 sprigs of parsley
3 eggs, beaten
  Garlic powder
  Salt and pepper to taste
  Peanut oil

Soak chick peas overnight in cold water or you can buy cooked chickpeas in the can. Remove skins and drain. Grind chick peas with the bread, hot pepper and parsley through a food grinder. Add eggs, mixing well, then the seasonings. Set mixture aside for one hour; this lets the flavors permeate. Make into balls about an inch in diameter then mash slightly so that they are just flat enough to fry but still nicely rounded. Or it can be cooked as a mix and served in Arab or Greek pocket bread (see Index) rather than as patties. Fry in peanut oil to brown on both sides.

SAUCE

1 cup canned tomato sauce
1 hot pepper, finely chopped
  Salt to taste

Be sure to use tomato sauce, not puree or paste; the latter two have a sweeter taste rather than a tangy one. Mix ingredients together and simmer for 10 minutes. Spoon over falafel patties or into pocket bread over falafel mixture.

LATKES (Potato Pancakes)

2 eggs, beaten
3 cups grated raw potatoes, drained
4 tablespoons grated onion
2 tablespoons cracker or matso meal
1 teaspoon salt
  Pinch baking powder
¼ teaspoon pepper
½ cup butter

Using the fine or medium side on your hand grater, grate peeled potatoes to a measure of three full cups. Beat the eggs and add the well-drained grated potatoes, then the onion, salt, pepper and meal. Heat half of the butter in frying pan and drop the potato mixture into the hot butter by tablespoons. Fry until golden brown on both sides. Keep latkes hot in the heated oven until all are fried. Add more butter to frying pan as needed. This recipe makes 8 pancakes which are usually served two to a person. Top with apple sauce, sour cream or yogurt, or fresh fruit or cheese.

JERUSALEM SALAD

1 9-oz. package frozen artichoke hearts
1 6-oz. package of Italian salad dressing mix
   Salad oil
   Water
1 cup thinly sliced mushrooms
1 3-oz. package of Kosher or vegetarian gelatin mix (agar agar) of lemon flavor
1 tablespoon diced red pimentos (buy in tiny jar)
1 cup real mayonnaise (do not substitute salad dressing)

Early in the day, or the day before serving, prepare the artichoke hearts according to package directions; drain and cool slightly. Cut artichokes in half and set aside.

Prepare the Italian salad dressing mix as given on label. In a large bowl combine salad dressing, artichokes and sliced mushrooms; refrigerate for an hour. Drain artichoke mixture after chilled, but reserve the dressing in which they soaked in refrigerator. Meanwhile, prepare the gelatin as directed on package but using only 1¾ cups of water; refrigerate until the consistency of unbeaten egg white. Fold in the artichoke mixture and the pimento. Pour

into a 4-cup mold, cover and refrigerate until firm. In a small bowl with a fork, combine mayonnaise and the reserved Italian dressing. Unmold gelatin onto platter garnished with Bibb lettuce and serve with mayonnaise mixture as dressing.

BEETS WITH HORSERADISH

2 cups grated cooked beets
4 tablespoons grated horseradish
2 teaspoons sugar
1 teaspoon salt
1 teaspoon vinegar
2 tablespoons salad oil

Mix ingredients together and chill for two hours. This is served as a relish dish to pass and let each diner help himself.

SOUR CREAM BATTER FOR BLINTZES

1 egg
¼ cup milk
¾ cup commercial sour cream
⅛ teaspoon salt
1 cup all purpose flour, sifted

Beat egg, then beat milk into egg. Stir in sour cream and salt, then stir in flour last, mixing until smooth.

Heat butter in a 6- or 7-inch skillet, pour about 2 tablespoons of the batter into it, tilting and turning to spread batter evenly. Fry until browned then turn and brown other side. This batter makes a rich pancake, more suitable for sweet fillings. Fill each blintz with a heaping tablespoon of filling, and roll up each one and arrange them in a buttered baking dish. Bake in 450°F. oven for 10 minutes. Serve with a dollop of sour cream on top.

BLINTZ FILLINGS
Apple Filling

1 egg white
1½ cups apples finely chopped
4 tablespoons sugar
½ teaspoon cinnamon
3 tablespoons brown sugar
3 tablespoons melted butter

Beat the egg white until it begins to stiffen. Fold in apples, sugar and cinnamon. Fill the blintzes and arrange in a buttered baking pan. Sprinkle with brown sugar and butter. Bake in 400°F. oven for 20 minutes. Makes about 18.

Blueberry Filling

1½ cups blueberries
3 tablespoons sugar
⅛ teaspoon nutmeg
1 tablespoon cornstarch

Mix all ingredients together, roll in blintz and bake as apple filled ones.

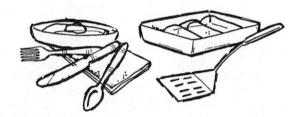

ITALY

Italian cooking is so distinctive and there are so very many variations of these national dishes, that we felt a single menu would slight the reader. So, rather than give you one single meal, we are offering instead a veritable Joseph's Feast of dishes from which you can choose your own, adding to it the Antipasto and Bread Sticks, to make your own Italian feast.

ANTIPASTO TRAY

Arrange greens of your choice on large platter or tray. In sections on the tray, with attention to color and size, arrange tiny pickled beets left whole; roasted Italian sweet peppers (purchased in jars but remember to rinse under cold water before serving); ripe olives stuffed with almonds; radish roses; skinned tomato quarters; button mushrooms, artichoke hearts; stuffed hard cooked eggs with minced scallion tops and mayonnaise and parsley garnish; celery root cut in julienne strips; carrot sticks; tiny pearl pickled onions. You may add other things if you like, such as thin slices of cheese curled into cornucopias. Antipasto literally means 'before the pasta' and it is served first, as an appetizer or relish tray.

BREAD STICKS

1 package active dry yeast
⅔ cup warm water
2 tablespoons of salad oil
2 tablespoons olive oil
1 teaspoon salt
1 tablespoon sugar
2¼ cups unsifted flour
1 egg, beaten
　 Poppy seeds or sesame seeds (optional)

Dissolve yeast in warm water; add oils, salt, sugar, and one cup of the flour. Beat until smooth. Add enough of the remaining flour to make a stiff dough. Turn out on a floured board and knead until smooth and elastic—about 5 minutes—using additional flour as needed. Place dough in a buttered bowl, cover with a damp cloth, and let rise in warm place (about 80°) until doubled in size which is about 1 hour. Punch dough down and divide in half. Cut each half into 24 equal pieces. Roll each, using the palms of the hands, into 6 to 8 inch lengths. Place these thin rolls on greased baking sheets about ½ inch apart. Brush with egg and sprinkle with seeds, if desired. Let rise in warm place for 30 minutes. Bake in moderate slow oven, about 325° F., for 30 minutes or until golden brown.

ZUCCHINI PUFF

3 tablespoons butter
⅓ cup grated onion
½ teaspoon salt
¼ teaspoon thyme, crushed
1½ cups grated zucchini
2 eggs, separated
¼ cup milk
¼ cup grated Parmesan cheese
¼ cup crushed crackers

If zucchini is young and tender do not peel it but grate it whole. Melt butter in a saucepan and add the grated onion to it; cook until onion is transparent. Remove from fire and add salt and thyme, the egg yolks beaten, milk, cheese and crackers. Next add in the grated cheese and zucchini and mix well. Beat the egg whites until stiff and fold into mixture. Pour into well-buttered 6 x 8 x 2-inch baking dish and bake at 350°F. for 35 to 40 minutes or until brown. You may like to drizzle a little melted butter and a bit more Parmesan cheese on the top before baking. Serves 4 to 6.

ASPARAGUS PARMIGIANA

1 bunch fresh asparagus heads
1 quart water
1 tablespoon salt
¾ cup Parmesan cheese, freshly grated
Butter

Select your asparagus carefully choosing full heads and wash the asparagus thoroughly and cut off the lower part of the stalk and throw away. With a knife scrape the lower half of each edible stalk, taking care not to damage the heads. Place in fast boiling water with no lid.

Use 1 level tablespoon of salt per quart of water, as asparagus does not take up salt as readily as other vegetables. It is best to use a flat surface pan or flame resistant flat dish for boiling the asparagus. Cook for 15 to 20 minutes. Remove asparagus carefully with a spatula, drain and place in a buttered shallow baking dish. Freshly grated Parmesan cheese is now sprinkled over the top and dot with butter. Bake in a 350°F. oven long enough for the cheese to brown and become a little crisp on top. If you have hungry guests, double this recipe, as it is very tasty and usually very popular. It is often served as an entrée after antipasto and soup.

This dish is attractive served in individual flat white au gratin (oven-resistant) dishes. This style of small platter for individual servings is popular in European countries.

BROCCOLI ITALIENNE

1 fresh bunch of broccoli in enough salted water to steam it.
4 tablespoons butter
4 tablespoons flour
4 to 6 hardcooked eggs, sliced
½ teaspoon salt
2 cups milk
1 clove garlic, crushed
⅛ teaspoon fresh ground pepper
½ cup freshly grated Parmesan cheese

Take one bunch of broccoli and cut stems about 4 inches below the flower and discard bottom parts. Use all the smaller leaves and all the little sprouts which you find where larger stalks join. Chop tops and stalks into very fine pieces. Steam or blanch briefly in salted boiling water, for 5 minutes, drain well.

Make a white sauce of butter, flour, milk and salt over a low fire, stirring until sauce thickens. Add garlic clove, pepper and cook additional 3 to 5 minutes until the flour taste has left the sauce. Add ½ cup grated Parmesan cheese to sauce. Place well-drained broccoli in individual au gratin dishes and place one sliced hardcooked egg on each dish. Pour sauce over it, then sprinkle with bread crumbs. Bake at 375°F. until cheese melts and browns. Serve in au gratin dishes on plates. Broccoli is rich in potassium and Vitamin B.

CAPONATA

½ cup olive oil
2 cups diced celery
1 medium eggplant, cut in cubes ¾-inch square
1 large onion, chopped
⅓ cup wine vinegar
1 can (2¼ oz.) sliced ripe olives, drained
1 teaspoon sugar
2 large tomatoes, peeled and diced
1 cup water
1 tablespoon capers, drained
¼ cup sliced green olives stuffed with pimentos
2 tablespoons minced parsley
Salt to taste

This is a Sicilian dish and is served as an appetizer, or mounded on a bed of greens as a first course with crusty Italian bread. It is best made a day ahead of time to allow flavors to blend. You can store, covered tightly, for as long as a week.

Heat olive oil in large frying pan. Do not substitute other oil as olive oil lends a particular taste to the dish. Add celery and cook till tender (about 7 minutes), stirring often. Remove celery from pan with slotted spoon and set aside. Add eggplant to the pan and cook over medium heat, stirring until it is lightly browned and tender (about 10 minutes). Add onion and continue cooking and stirring until onion is soft but not browned. Lift eggplant and onion out with slotted spoon and set aside. Add vinegar, sugar, tomatoes and water to the pan. Cook over medium heat, again stirring, until a fairly smooth sauce is formed; this is about five minutes as a rule.

Return other mixtures to the pan with the sauce. Stir in the capers, olives and parsley and simmer about 20 minutes longer. Taste to see if additional salt is needed. This is usually served at room temperature, so if it has been refrigerated before, remove in time to let it warm up. Serves 6.

MUSHROOM TETRAZINNI

1 package (16 oz.) spaghettini
2 6-oz. packages of provolone cheese slices
6 tablespoons butter
½ lb. mushrooms cut in thick slices
1 chopped onion
3 tablespoons all-purpose flour
1½ teaspoons salt
Dash of pepper
2 cups milk
⅓ cup chopped parsley

About 40 minutes before serving, cook the spaghettini according to label instructions. Drain. Cut cheese slices into small pieces, and reserve ½ cup for topping. Preheat the broiler. In a 3-quart saucepan melt and heat the butter to sauté onion and mushrooms until tender. Stir in the flour, salt and pepper until blended. Gradually stir in the milk. Next, add the cheese and parsley and cook, stirring constantly, until mixture is thickened and cheese is melted. Place the hot, drained spaghettini in a large, oven-proof dish and pour the sauce over it. Sprinkle the top with the reserved ½ cup of cheese pieces and broil until cheese is melted. Serves 4.

MACARONI SHELLS AND SPINACH

- 1 package shell macaroni (12 oz.)
- 2 packages (each 10 oz.) frozen chopped spinach
- 1 cup oil
- 2 large chopped onions
- 2 cups Ricotta cheese
- ½ cup Parmesan cheese, freshly grated
- 2 eggs, slightly beaten
- 1½ teaspoons dill weed
- 1 teaspoon salt
- ½ teaspoon pepper

Thaw the spinach and squeeze as dry as possible. Sauté onions in oil lightly. Mix all the above ingredients together and set aside while preparing the dill sauce.

DILL SAUCE

- 8 tablespoons butter
- 8 tablespoons flour
- 5 cups milk
- 1½ tablespoons dill weed
- 1 teaspoon salt
- ½ teaspoon white pepper

Melt butter and add flour, stirring. Then add milk, stirring constantly until mixture thickens and starchy taste is gone. Add dill, salt and pepper.

Cover bottom of a shallow (2-quart) pyrex baking dish with 2 cups of the dill sauce. Spread the spinach mixture over the layer of sauce and sprinkle the top with Parmesan cheese. Cover spinach and cheese layer with remaining dill sauce. If you like, you can again sprinkle the top with Parmesan and even a few bread crumbs, but it is optional. Cover dish with foil and bake at 350° for one hour. Serves 6 to 8.

ARTICHOKE SPAGHETTI SAUCE
(Salsa du Carciofi)

- 3 tablespoons olive oil
- 1 tablespoon butter
- 3 medium Jerusalem artichokes, sliced very thin
- 1 medium onion sliced thin
- ½ clove garlic, minced
- 2 cups canned Italian-style tomatoes
- 1 bay leaf
- ½ teaspoon dried basil
  Salt
  Pepper

Heat olive oil and butter in a saucepan. Cook artichokes for three minutes. Add the onion, garlic, tomatoes, bay leaf, basil, salt and pepper. Simmer covered, stirring occasionally, until artichokes are tender. Makes enough sauce for about 1 pound of spaghetti.

SWEET BASIL MACARONI

1 pkg. (8 oz.) elbow macaroni
¼ cup minced fresh basil leaves (or 2 tablespoons dried sweet basil soaked in 1 tablespoon water)
2 tablespoons minced parsley
1 clove garlic, crushed in press
  Coarse ground black pepper
1 tablespoon melted butter
¼ cup olive oil
2 tablespoons freshly grated Parmesan cheese
½ teaspoon salt
½ teaspoon nutmeg
  Dash chili powder
½ cup hot water
  Parmesan cheese

This is a simple family pasta seasoned with more than the usual amount of sweet basil. If you like subtle seasonings, use only half the amount of basil indicated.

Cook macaroni in boiling salted water as directed on package. If you have a mortar and pestle, crush the basil, parsley and garlic together; put into a small saucepan. Mix in the olive oil, butter, 2 tablespoons Parmesan cheese, the other seasonings and ½ cup hot water. Over low heat, while draining the macaroni, thoroughly heat the mixture. Heap the pasta on a warm platter and pour sauce over the top. Sprinkle top with pepper and more Parmesan cheese. Serve immediately. Serves 4 to 6.

RIGATI-EGGPLANT BAKE

1 large eggplant, about 2 pounds
½ cup olive oil
1 pkg. rigati, ziti, or elbow macaroni
1 large onion, chopped (about 1 cup
1 24-ounce jar marinara sauce
1 15-oz. container Ricotta cheese, or cream-style cottage cheese
½ cup chopped parsley
1 teaspoon Italian dressing
1 pkg. (6 oz.) sliced Provolone cheese

Trim ends from eggplant, pare, and cut into ½-inch slices. Sauté slices a few at a time in part of the olive oil until soft. Drain on paper toweling until all are cooked and draining.

Cook rigati in a large kettle according to package directions; drain and return to empty kettle.

Sauté onion until soft, using same skillet used for eggplant; stir in marinara sauce and simmer until piping hot. Pour onion and sauce over rigati and blend well.

In small bowl, combine Ricotta cheese parsley and Italian dressing. In a shallow, 12-cup baking dish place half the rigati in sauce in it, then add half the eggplant slices, overlapping them. Next add the cheese mixture, spreading evenly. Follow it by another layer of rigati mixture and top with remaining eggplant.

Bake in moderate oven (350°F.) for 20 minutes. Cut Provolone cheese into strips and arrange over top of eggplant and replace dish in oven for another 10 minutes or until cheese melts and mixture is bubbly hot.

RISSOTTO AI FUNCHI
(Rice with Mushrooms)

2 cups white unpolished rice
2 large onions, chopped fine
1 large can pear-shaped Italian tomatoes
   (approx. 12 oz.)
2 cups Italian dried mushrooms
2 cups tomato juice
6 oz. freshly grated Parmesan cheese
½ pound butter (not margarine)
1 teaspoon salt
⅛ teaspoon freshly ground pepper

Prepare mushrooms by pouring boiling water over them and allow to soak for 3 to 4 hours, changing the water 2 or 3 times. Strain and chop into very small pieces. In a large frying pan melt half a cup of butter over medium heat and sauté finely chopped onions until golden brown. Add uncooked rice and turn over thoroughly to mix with butter and onions. Cook for about a minute to heat the rice thoroughly, but keep turning to prevent rice from sticking. Add canned tomatoes you've cut into small chunks. Continue to add juice from canned tomatoes, then tomato juice in addition to that so as to keep a layer of juice on top of rice, just covering it. Rice absorbs the liquid and has a tendency to stick so you must keep adding juice and stirring. If you still need more liquid, you can add a little boiling water, but use care to not add too much liquid just before rice is finished.

When rice is finished cooking, it should be allowed to absorb all the excess liquid. Five minutes before serving, while still over the heat, sprinkle grated Parmesan cheese over the mixture. Mix in well. Parmesan is also served at the table in separate dish for each guest to help themselves.

BAKED LASAGNE

3 tablespoons olive oil
1 cup minced onions
1 cup green peppers, sliced thin and
   chopped
2 cloves garlic, crushed
1½ teaspoons salt
¼ teaspoon pepper
   Pinch of thyme
4 oz. Peccorino cheese
1½ teaspoons dried basil
2 tablespoons parsley, chopped
1 can plum tomatoes, Italian style peeled
1 can (8 oz.) heavy tomato paste
½ pound Parmesan cheese
½ pound lasagne noodles, 1½" wide
¾ pound Mozzarella cheese
1½ pounds Ricotta cheese

Heat olive oil and sauté onions, green pepper, seasonings. Add drained tomatoes, reserving juice, but add in by stirring vigorously to prevent sticking, the puree. Then add the reserve juice as needed only, as this sauce should remain thick. Cover and simmer for 30 minutes.

Cook lasagne by package directions. Drain. Spread about one-third of the sauce on the bottom of a 12 x 8 pyrex baking dish, then spread alternate layers of the lasagne, Mozzorella, Ricotta and sprinkle with Parmesan and half of the remaining sauce. Repeat the layers until all ingredients are used. Cover the remaining sauce and sprinkle again with Parmesan. Bake in oven at 350° for 35 minutes. Serve hot. Serves 8.

RICOTTA CHEESE PANCAKES

1 cup Ricotta cheese
3 eggs
2 tablespoons salad oil
¼ cup all-purpose flour
   Soft butter
2 tablespoons sugar
¼ teaspoon salt
2 cups fresh or frozen raspberries
   Powdered sugar

In a blender jar, combine eggs, ricotta, flour, salt, sugar and salad oil. Fill blender only ¼ full at a time and hold cover down securely. Whirl until smooth. With a rubber spatula push ingredients from side of blender. Some people prefer to push or rub the ricotta through a wire strainer and then beat with remaining ingredients until they get a smooth mixture.

Dip tablespoons of batter to make 3-inch rounds on a lightly buttered griddle or cast iron frying pan over a medium-low heat. Turn cakes with spatula when bubbles form on the surface. When browned lightly on both sides, remove and keep warm until all are cooked.

Serve dusted with powdered sugar and fresh raspberries on top. This makes a delicious entrée when a light meal or brunch is to be served.

PEACH MELBA

1 package lemon flavored vegetarian gelatin
½ fresh or canned peach for each serving or mold
½ pint (1 cup) whipped cream
   Sugar
1 teaspoon pure almond extract

Prepare the gelatin according to the package instructions. If you are using separate gelatine molds, place ½ peach (fresh peeled or canned) in each mold; if you are using 1 large mold, place the halves around that evenly. Pour the lemon gelatin over the peach halves and chill. Whip the heavy cream, adding sugar to taste, and the 1 teaspoon of almond extract. Top each serving with the flavored whipped cream and serve.

FRUIT RHAPSODY

   Red grapes
   Orange section slices (or canned
   Mandarin sections
   Blueberries
   Strawberries
   Cantaloupe small wedges, peeled
   Honeydew Melon small wedges, peeled
   Fresh mint leaves

Topaz Dressing:

1 tablespoon grated orange rind
¼ cup shredded coconut
1 cup mayonnaise
½ cup whipped cream

Clean and prepare the fresh fruit; combine in large, pretty serving dish.

Make the Topaz Dressing and pour over the fruit. Serve in the large dish, allowing each guest to help himself in smaller matching bowls.

HOMEMADE BISCUIT TORTONI

½ cup sugar
¼ cup water (about 5 tablespoons)
3 egg yolks
½ pint (1 cup) whipped cream
1 teaspoon pure orange extract, or
1 teaspoon pure vanilla
½ cup fresh macaroons, crumbled
1 tablespoon of caramel
Almonds, browned and chopped fine

Make a golden parfait by boiling ½ cup sugar and ¼ cup water for 5 minutes from the time it begins to boil. Beat 3 egg yolks until thick and lemon color. Pour the golden syrup into the egg yolks, stirring constantly with a large spoon while pouring.

When the mixture has cooled completely, add ½ pint of whipped cream and 1 teaspoon flavoring into the mixture; folding it in gently until it is completely mixed and blended.

Spoon into parfait glasses or small paper cups and freeze in the refrigerator for 3 hours.

While the parfait mixture is chilling, you can prepare the toppings of caramel and crumbled macaroons. If you have no caramel, you can easily make it by caramelizing sugar. Place 2 tablespoons granulated sugar in a bright, clean frying pan. Shake the pan back and forth until all the sugar is brown, but not burnt. Remove from the pan to cool. It will be hard, but add 1 tablespoon cooking sherry and allow caramel sugar to dissolve.

Pound ½ cup fresh macaroons into crumb size and sprinkle the caramel into the crumbs. Top each container with the caramel macaroon crumbs and serve with an additional topping of finely chopped, browned almonds.

JAMAICA

Jamaica Dinner
Tall, Cool Iced Tea with Mint
Dill Dip Tray
Vegetable Nut Loaf with Mushroom Sauce
Olive Stuffed Tomatoes
Grapefruit Ginger Mold with
Fluffy Fruit Dressing
Orange-Glazed Bananas with Ice Cream

ICED TEA WITH MINT

Some teas, even of high quality, are not satisfactory for iced tea because the infusion becomes cloudy when cold. Among black teas, English Breakfast (China Congou) is a good choice for iced tea. Formosa Oolong is the best selection from its group.

Double the portion of tea to water in making iced tea. If the ice supply is unlimited, the freshly made hot tea may be strained directly over cracked ice in tall glasses. Otherwise the tea should be poured from the leaves after the usual steeping period, cooled without refrigeration, and iced just before serving.

If the tea becomes cloudy on cooling, stir in a little boiling water to clear it. To ice instant tea, mix 2 level teaspoons with cold water in a tall glass; add ice. Float a marachino cherry and a mint leaf to glass with a thin lemon slice balancing on the rim.

Serve extra fine granulated sugar for this purpose. Each guest will help themselves to the sugar bowl. Each glass should be accompanied with a long tea glass spoon.

DILL DIP TRAY

Dip:
- 1 cup commercial sour cream
- 1 tablespoon chopped fresh parsley
- 1 tablespoon chopped scallions
- 1 teaspoon dill weed
- ¼ teaspoon onion powder
- ¼ teaspoon celery salt
- 1 cup mayonnaise (no substitute)

Tray:
- 1 or 2 fresh zucchini
- 1 small white head cauliflower
- 2 or 3 carrots
- 4 stalks celery

Blend sour cream and mayonnaise together. Do not use salad dressing or any substitute for the real mayonnaise. Add seasonings. Wash, drain the vegetables by separating cauliflower into small flowerettes, make sticks of carrots and celery, and cut thin round slices of the firm, dark-skinned zucchini. Arrange on tray with rye crackers and corn chips for those who do not care for raw vegetables.

JAMAICA VEGETABLE NUT LOAF

3 onions, chopped
1 cup diced celery
1 green pepper, chopped
1 cup walnuts
4 or 5 carrots
  Cracker crumbs
4 tablespoons oil
4 slices bread
1 or 2 eggs, depending on size
½ teaspoon thyme
  Salt and pepper to taste

Sauté chopped onions, celery and green pepper in about 4 tablespoons of oil for a few minutes. Do not brown. Run carrots, bread and nuts through a food grinder and add them to the vegetables in a large skillet. Add beaten eggs and seasonings. Put mixture in oiled loaf pan and sprinkle the top with crushed cracker crumbs. Bake in 350° oven for 40 minutes, or until brown. This loaf can be served with either mushroom or tomato sauce. Serves 4.

MUSHROOM SAUCE

1 cup white cream sauce
1 cup chopped fresh mushrooms
1 tablespoon catsup
1 tablespoon butter
1 tablespoon fresh lemon juice
2 teaspoons A-1 or Worcestershire Sauce
1 teaspoon fresh paprika

Make white cream sauce first in the usual way—1 tablespoon butter melted in pan, stir in 2 tablespoons flour and add 1 cup water or ½ cup water and ½ cup milk. Cook, stirring until sauce thickens.

In a small skillet, sauté the mushroom pieces in the tablespoon of butter until slightly brown. Add the sauteed mushrooms and the residual butter to the white sauce; cook over low heat, stirring, for about 10 minutes. Stir in the other ingredients one at a time to blend. Continue over heat for another minute, until it is warmed through. Stir and serve as an accompaniment to various vegetarian loaves and patties.

OLIVE-STUFFED TOMATOES

6 firm tomatoes
½ green pepper, peeled and chopped
1 small onion, chopped
  Salt and pepper to taste
1 cup pitted ripe olives
3 tablespoons bread crumbs, torn in very tiny bits
1 teaspoon sugar

Hollow out 6 firm tomatoes. In butter fry the peeled and chopped green pepper and chopped onion for about 10 minutes. Add the scooped-out tomato pulp and the chopped ripe olives. Add 3 tablespoons of bread crumbs, the sugar and salt and pepper to taste. Stuff the tomatoes with the mixture. Arrange in pan, oiled or buttered, and bake for 25 mintes in oven at 375°. Serve immediately on thin slices of toast points, or cut the bread into large circles and toast. Serves 4 to 6.

GRAPEFRUIT GINGER MOLD

2 cans (1 lb.) grapefruit sections, unsweetened variety
2 packages (3 oz.) vegetarian lemon gelatin
¾ cup boiling water
¾ cup lemon juice
2 cups ginger ale
1 medium red apple, diced
½ cup diced celery
2 to 3 tablespoons finely chopped Crystallized ginger candy
Lettuce to line serving dish
1 avocado, peeled and sliced

Drain grapefruit, reserving the liquid. Dissolve the gelatin in boiling water. Follow directions on package closely, as gelatins free from animal tissue have a different timing to jell. Add grapefruit sections, lemon juice and ginger ale. Chill until slightly thickened. Add the remaining ingredients. Pour into a 2-quart salad ring or mold; refrigerate for several hours. Turn out molded gelatin onto a very large platter you have garnished with salad greens. Arrange avocado slices around the mold and sprinkle them with lemon juice to prevent browning. Serve with Fluffy Fruit Salad Dressing.

FLUFFY FRUIT SALAD DRESSING

2 eggs, slightly beaten
½ cup sugar
⅓ cup orange juice
1 teaspoon grated orange rind
2 cups dairy sour cream

Mix together the eggs, sugar and orange juice in a small saucepan and cook over medium heat, stirring constantly until thickened. Blend in orange juice and orange rind. Cool. Gently fold in sour cream. Cover and chill for at least 2 hours. Serve in a glass bowl and allow guests to help themselves. This dressing is especially good over fruit salads.

ORANGE-GLAZED BANANAS WITH ICE CREAM

6 bananas, peeled
¾ brown sugar, firmly packed
¼ cup butter (not margarine)
½ cup orange juice
1 tablespoon grated orange peel
2 teaspoons chopped candied ginger
Juice of ½ lemon

Peel bananas and halve lengthwise. Arrange in a shallow baking dish such as an au gratin platter. Place cut side up and brush with lemon juice.

Mix together the butter, brown sugar, orange juice and grated peel with the candied ginger. Place the flame resistant platter about 8 inches below the flame in broiler and baste with syrup. Watch carefully, occasionally basting with syrup. This can be baked rather than broiled, by placing in a 375° oven for 15 minutes or until the bananas are glazed brown, basting once or twice with the syrup. In the broiler it takes from 5 to 7 minutes.

For each serving arrange two banana halves on a dessert plate and top with vanilla ice cream. Spoon hot sauce over it.

JAPAN

Japanese Dinner
Miso Soup (clear soup with Bean Curd)
Tempura
Oriental Eggs   Green Beans in Custard
Kuri Rice (Chestnut Rice)
Sukiyaki
Tea

In Oriental meals, all food items are brought to the table at one time. The soup, in a small bowl with a cover, may be sipped during the entire meal. The guests participate in preparing their own portions and help themselves to dishes on the table. A hibachi, or patio style barbeque grill, is used.

Miso Soup

1 quart of vegetarian soup stock
¼ cup of miso (bean curd)
¼ teaspoon salt
1 egg, beaten
    Twist of orange or lemon peel for each serving
    Chopped chives

Prepare 1 quart of vegetarian soup stock, mixed with ¼ cup of miso and salt. Beat 1 egg and while swirling soup in the kettle, gradually trickle the beaten egg into it. In each soup bowl place a twist of citrus peel, then pour or ladle soup over it. Sprinkle top with chopped chives and serve immediately. Serves 4 to 6 people.

TEMPURA

There are legends as to the origin and meaning of "Tempura". One is that it was named after its Buddhist originator who centuries ago created the dish to please his noble Lord. The cooking is quick, about 4-5 minutes, as each person dips his selection of vegetables into the batter first then quickly deep-frying it in hot vegetable oil. Peanut oil is probably the best as it does not smoke as badly when very hot. Raw ingredients are quantities to give each person.

3 green pepper rings about ¼ inch thick
3 slices unpeeled zucchini, sliced lengthwise ¼ inch think
3 tender string beans
3 sliced large mushrooms
3 slices sweet potato (keep fresh in water to prevent discoloration, and pat dry before dipping into batter)
3 slices Japanese eggplant
    Chinese turnip, cabbage, carrot sticks or any other vegetable can also be used

Any other vegetable that appeals to you that can cook in 4-5 minutes.

Make your batter at least 15 minutes before you need it, but it can be prepared an hour ahead which is more convenient. Each cook has his own combination. Basic batter recipe follows:

1 cup flour
1 cup water (adjust so batter is like whip cream)
1 egg
A dash of salt
1 teaspoon sugar (acts as a browning agent)
½ teaspoon baking powder (this gives more flavor to the vegetables)

You may use Chinese chopsticks which, being longer, are more satisfactory for the preparation of this dish. The cook should have two pairs, one that does not touch the oil which is for the batter, and one for turning the food and removing from the oil. Do not over-mix; the batter will be a bit lumpy. It will thicken after sitting in refrigerator. If so, add only a bit of water and mix with chopsticks to which batter should cling and flow off in large drops. You can mix all together with an egg beater. This is an attractive dish; the baking powder makes the batter puff up and gives a lacy effect.

Heat oil. Peanut oil is best, as it does not smoke as some oils do. Test for right temperature, 375° F., by dropping a ball of batter into the oil. If it settles to the bottom, the oil is not hot enough and the 'tempura' will be soggy and oily. If it sizzles on the top, the oil is too hot and the 'tempura' will burn without properly cooking inside. If the drop of batter falls to the bottom of the fry pan and remains only an instant, then rises to the surface and sizzles gently, the temperature of the batter is just right. Maintain the heat while frying. The more oil in the pan, the easier it will be to maintain the proper temperature.

Have prepared ahead of time a basic dipping sauce which is given in the "Sukiyaki Sauce" recipe. To this can be added grated Japanese radish or American radish and/or grated ginger for a different taste.

Tempura properly prepared must be cooked immediately, and served while it is still fresh, hot and crispy and served a little at a time to be enjoyed. The reason for cooking on the table is so the hostess can be with her guests; otherwise, the cook has to remain in the kitchen. Though the Japanese do not eat sweets after the meal as we Americans or Europeans are accustomed to doing, you may peel and cut into chunks either apples, pears, pineapple, or bananas (use green ones, very firm) for tempura while all the accoutrements are handy.

Fruit for 4
Tempura Batter
Powdered Sugar
Oil for Frying

Dip chunks into batter and fry as you would tempura. Drain on paper toweling, saving the oil for future use in a cool place. If covered, it can be saved for several weeks. Sprinkle with sugar and serve immediately, while hot. Serve on separate plates for each guest along with tea.

ORIENTAL EGGS
(Meat substitute served with tempura)

8 eggs
⅓ cup light cream

½ teaspoon garlic salt
⅛ teaspoon pepper
2 tablespoons butter
1 bunch scallions, green tops removed
1 tablespoon soya sauce
⅛ teaspoon ground ginger
1 5-oz. can water chestnuts, drained and sliced thin
1 cup halved cherry tomatoes

This scrambled egg dish topped with fresh tomato sauce is similar to a Basque piperade, but has some surprising additions. In a bowl combine 8 eggs, ⅓ cup light cream, ½ teaspoon garlic salt, ⅛ teaspoon pepper. Beat until well blended, then set aside.

Melt 1 tablespoon of butter in a frying pan and sauté only the white part of a bunch of scallions, just until soft, but not browned. Add 1 tablespoon soy sauce. (Kikkoman Shoyu Co. Ltd. Product of Japan is far superior to domestic ones. It is the only brand widely available in the U.S. that is actually made and aged in the proper way, and there is a vast difference in taste of the domestic substitute ones). Add ⅛ teaspoon ground ginger, 1 5-oz. can water chestnuts, drained and sliced thin, 1 cup halved cherry tomatoes. Stir gently until heated; tomatoes should not lose their shape.

Meanwhile, melt the remaining 1 tablespoon butter in a frying pan. Add the egg mixture and cook, stirring just until softly scrambled. Turn eggs on a warm platter. If necessary, increase heat under tomato mixture to evaporate excess liquid quickly; serve over eggs which are spooned over hot rice. If you have individual shallow "au-gratin" white platters used by the European and Oriental countries, use by all means. They are so useful as each guest is then able to be served hot food. Never heat these dishes when they are empty, but fill individually and cook in them if baking.

GREEN BEANS IN CUSTARD

This is a simple dish that is elegant. It is substantial enough to be an entrée for a lunch or is simple enough to be a side dish.

1 lb. fresh or frozen string beans
½ cup vegetarian stock
2 tablespoons soy sauce
Dash Salt
4 eggs

Cut beans any style you like. Parboil in stock and soy sauce until just tender. Beat eggs but not to a froth. Place all items (including stock) into a bowl or pot that can be put into a steamer and steam until custard is set, about 8 to 10 minutes. Serve hot. Fresh or frozen peas can be cooked in the same manner. Serve with hot rice.

KURI RICE (Chestnut Rice)

3 cups dry rice
4 cups water
15 to 20 peeled chestnuts, cut into chunks
2 tablespoons soy sauce
Dash of salt
2 teaspoons sugar or "mirin" (sweetened rice wine)

Wash rice. Add all ingredients, cover and cook as steamed rice. If served as an entrée, should be served with pickles or a vegetable. You can peel chestnuts easily by making an incision with a knife and boiling them for five minutes, or you can make an incision and roast them for 30 minutes or so, and peel them. Baking gives another pleasant dimension to the chestnut rice.

JAPAN'S SUKIYAKI
(Pronounced S'kee-áh-kee)

Can be served a-la-vegetarian over crisply steamed or sautéed vegetables. Prepare the following items, each in its own "stack." If you don't have all of them don't fret; one or two won't be sorely missed. Except for your main vegetables which can be cauliflowerettes, all others should be Julienned, that is cut in shoestring strips—such as string beans, mushrooms, bamboo shoots, carrots, broccoli, brussel sprouts, spinach, turnips (Daikon), onions or scallions. Vegetables may be combined or used singly. To get the proper flavor it is suggested that vegetables with which you use the following topping be cooked and served hot, with plain rice served in a separate bowl, which gives a real Japanese look.

SUKIYAKI SAUCE

Amounts are adjusted as to the number of guests to be served.

1 cup vegetarian stock
½ cup sugar
½ cup soy sauce
Peanut oil

Use a well insulated electric hot-plate to protect the table, and to further protect the table you can fold newspaper to a thickness of ½ inch to set the hotplate on. Your sukiyaki pan should be very heavy cast iron and 8 to 10 inches in diameter. Chopsticks are used to handle the vegetables while sautéing them, and they are smaller than Chinese chopsticks and therefore easier to manage. Use 2 tablespoons of oil for coating the pan and allow the oil to sizzle.

Add the vegetables, ⅓ each in their own "corner" of the pan, except for the 2" lengths of scallions.

Cook vegetables until just tender crisp, and bamboo shoots until just heated. Serve over rice.

SUPAINO DAIKON (Fresh vinegared daikon)

2 to 3 large daikon (about 3 lbs.)
1 cup water
1 cup sugar
⅓ cup vinegar
3 tablespoons salt

Peel the daikon (Japanese turnips) and slice crosswise in slices about ⅛" thick. Put in bowl or crock. Combine the remaining ingredients in a saucepan and bring to a boil. Pour this sauce over the sliced daikon, turn and cover, store in a cool place or in the refrigerator for 3 to 4 days.

MEXICO

Dinner Menu

Relish Plate of Green Onions, Green Stuffed Olives and Hot Chilies
(*Cebollas, Aceitunas and Chiles Picantes*)
Scrambled Egg Dish (*Chilaquiles*),
Sauteed Green Peppers and Sauteed Bananas
(*Pimientos Verdes Fritos, Platanos Fritos*)
El Rancho Salad with Guacamole Dressing
Guava Fruit Punch
Mexican Spiced Custard (*Jericalla*)

CHILAQUILES (Scrambled Egg Dish)
(Chee-la-keè-les)

There are many versions of this though all have crisp tortilla bits inside. The cooked mixture given here can stay creamy and fresh for about one hour kept at a warm temperature.

6   corn tortillas
2   tablespoons salad oil
4   tablespoons butter
½   cup minced onion
½   to 1 can (4 oz.) California green chili
     peppers, seeded and chopped
1   cup light cream
1   can (6 oz.) white sauce
8   eggs
1   teaspoon salt
10 or 12 vegetarian protein breakfast
     sausage links
3   tomatoes, peeled, seeded and chopped
2   cups shredded sharp cheddar cheese
     Stuffed olives (Aceitunas)
     Salsa de chile (red or green chili sauce)

Cut tortillas in matchstick size pieces. Heat salad oil and 2 tbs. butter in electric fry pan set at 350° F. Sauté tortillas until crisp, about 5 minutes. Leave in pan but pushed to one side. Melt remaining 2 tbs. butter and sauté onions and chilies for 4 minutes.

In a bowl, gradually stir cream into white sauce until smooth. Follow directions on can. Beat in eggs and salt with a fork. Immediately reduce heat of electric skillet to 250° and pour in eggs, stirring until softly scrambled, about 3 minutes. Mix tortilla pieces in with the eggs.

Arrange with browned breakfast links around, and garnish with chopped tomatoes, grated cheese and olives on top. Serve with chili sauce. Serves 6.

SAUTÉED GREEN PEPPERS

4   green bell peppers
2   tablespoons butter

Wash and seed the peppers, then sliver them. Heat butter in wide sauce pan, add peppers and cook over highest heat stirring frequently until peppers, though still bright green, are beginning to lose their crispness—about 5 minutes. Keep warm, not covered, until ready to serve. Serves 8.

SAUTÉED BANANAS
(Plátanos Fritos)

Allow 1 whole, firm, slightly green banana for each serving.

Melt ½ tablespoon butter per banana in a wide sauce pan over a medium-low heat. Peel bananas and cut in half lengthwise. Place cut-side down without crowding, and cook for about 10 minutes or until lightly browned. Carefully turn bananas with a wide spatula so as not to break them and cook another 5 to 7 minutes on that side. Keep bananas warm, uncovered, until ready to serve.

EL RANCHO SALAD

1   small head Iceberg lettuce, finely shredded
1   bunch scraped and thinly sliced radishes
½   bunch minced scallions
¼   pound Mexican cheese
3   medium tomatoes, peeled, seeded and chopped

Place the radishes, scallions and tomatoes on a bed of shredded lettuce, garnish with cheese and serve with corn chips. The Guacamole dressing is served to each guest to help himself.

GUACAMOLE DRESSING

1   clove of garlic
1   large or 2 medium avocados, halved, pitted and peeled
1   tablespoon lemon juice (or lime)
½   teaspoon salt
3   tablespoons grated onion
½   cup dairy sour cream
2   drops of liquid red pepper seasoning

Crush clove of garlic in bowl and rub bowl with it and discard. Drop in the avocado and mash with a fork. Sprinkle with lemon (or lime) juice and if you like, some of the finely chopped tomatoes from the salad ingredients above. Stir in salt, red pepper, onion, sour cream, and a small pinch of sugar. Mix gently and press the avocado pit into the dressing to help retain the color; cover and chill. Remove pit and stir before serving.

Add to the table decor by arranging a platter of fresh green onions, green chilies, and stuffed olives.

GUAVA FRUIT PUNCH

3   6 oz. cans frozen orange juice concentrate, reconstituted (9 cans of water)
3   cans (12 oz.) chilled guava nectar
2   unpeeled oranges, thinly sliced
1   pineapple, peeled, cored, cut in spears
1   large papaya, peeled and sliced
2   cups whole strawberries

Combine in punch bowl with pieces of fruit on top. This can be stretched with ginger ale, pineapple juice, or other beverage.

MEXICAN SPICED CUSTARD
("Jericalla — Hari-Ky-Yah")

2 cups milk
2 whole sticks of cinnamon (ea. 3 to 4 inches long)
½ cup sugar
3 whole large eggs, beaten

Combine milk, cinnamon sticks and sugar in a saucepan, stirring until it comes to a boil. Cover and chill overnight.

Set four small custard cups (ramekins) each at least ⅔ cup size, in a low square baking pan surrounded with the hottest tap water to about half the depth of the ramekins. Set this pan of water in a 350° oven. When oven has reached that desired temperature, again heat the milk mixture to scalding, stirring constantly. Set cinnamon sticks aside and slowly pour hot milk mixture into beaten eggs, mixing briskly with a fork. Pour an equal portion in each ramekin and set these dishes or cups in the hot water bath. Bake at 350° for 25 to 30 minutes, or until centers of the custards jiggle only slightly when a dish is shaken gently. Immediately remove custard cups from pan of water, using a wide spatula or kitchen tongs. Chill, and serve in same ramekins they were baked in. (If you like, rinse cinnamon sticks, and set ½ stick atop each Jericalla.) This is a refreshing dessert. Double recipe if needed. Serve with coffee.

MEXICAN SUPPER MENU
Mexican Enchiladas
Chiles Rellenos (Chesse-stuffed Green Chilies with Seasoned Tomato Sauce)
Steamed Rice
Frijoles Refritos (Refried Beans)
Fruit Basket

MEXICAN ENCHILADAS

⅓ cup flour
1 egg
   Milk
⅔ cup yellow corn meal
   Olive oil or cooking oil
   Salt

FILLING:

1 can protein meat substitute, diced
   coarsely
½ cup chopped green onions
1 can chopped ripe olives, or ½ 4-oz. can of
   chopped green chiles
¾ pound Monterey Jack cheese, grated

SAUCE:

1½ cups strong vegetarian bouillon
1½ cups dairy sour cream
   Monterey Jack cheese, grated
   Chopped onion

To make the tortillas, mix flour, yellow corn meal and salt to taste; add beaten egg and enough milk to make a very thin batter. Cook like thin pancakes in oil in a small (6- to 8- inch) frying pan. When done, fill with 1 heaping tablespoon of the filling and roll. Place in large, shallow, greased baking dish and sauce over them before serving.

The filling is made from 2 cups of the coarsely diced meat substitute mixed with ½ cup chopped green onions, sautéed lightly in oil. Add 1 can of chopped ripe olives or, if you prefer, half of a 4-oz. can of green chilies, to the mixture and then stir in half of the grated Monterey Jack cheese. Fill each tortilla with a tablespoon of this filling then roll up before placing in buttered casserole dish.

The sauce for these enchiladas is equally simple to make. Using 1½ cups of strong bouillon made from vegetarian cubes, gradually mix into 1½ cups sour cream and the Monterey Jack Cheese. Pour this sauce over the enchiladas in the baking dish and bake in a 300°F. oven for 30 minutes. Just before serving you may sparsely sprinkle the top of the bubbling hot enchiladas with chopped onions, or you may serve a side dish of them and one of grated cheese for each guest to help himself. Serves 4.

CHILES RELLENOS (Cheese-stuffed Green Chilies coated with Egg Batter)

6 canned whole green chilies (two 4-oz. cans)
6 strips (½" x ½" x 3") Monterey Jack cheese
   Flour
3 large eggs, separated
3 tablespoons flour
1 tablespoon water
¼ teaspoon salt
   Vegetable oil for frying

Rinse the chilies, pat dry with paper toweling and carefully remove all seeds found inside. Insert cheese strip inside each chili. Roll each stuffed chili in flour to coat all sides.

Beat egg whites in small bowl with electric mixer until soft peaks form. Beat egg yolks in a separate small bowl until fluffy and pale yellow—about 5 minutes. To the beaten egg yolks, add in 3 tablespoons flour, the water and salt and beat.

Heat ½ to 1 inch of oil in a small skillet to about 370°F. On a small saucer, place a lengthwise mound of the egg batter about ½ inch thick and 2 inches wide. Put a chili in the center and enclose it with more batter on the top.

Slice the batter-coated chili into hot oil and sauté for 4 minutes or until golden brown, turning it carefully with two slotted spoons or spatulas. Drain the fried relleno on paper toweling to remove excess oil. Keep them warm in a low oven until all are cooked. Serve hot with Seasoned Tomato Sauce (see next recipe) and sprinkle the top with chopped green scallions. Serves 6.

SEASONED TOMATO SAUCE

1   tablespoon vegetable shortening
¼   cup finely chopped green onions
1   clove garlic, minced
1   can (15 oz.) tomato sauce
½   teaspoon salt
½   teaspoon leaf oregano, crumbled

Heat vegetable oil in small saucepan. Add onions and minced garlic, sauté 1 minute. Stir in the tomato sauce, salt and oregano and heat thoroughly. Serve warm over Chiles Rellenos.

FRIJOLES (Refried Beans)

A meal is not a meal in Mexico unless beans are served in some form or other. The favorite bean dish is Frijoles Refritos, or refried beans.

2   cups Mexican pink beans
5   cups water
    Salt to taste
½   cup salad oil

Put the 2 cups of Mexican pink beans in 5 cups of lukewarm water and cook gently, covered, until tender—about 1½ to 2 hours. Add salt to taste during the last half hour of cooking. Be sure to stir the beans occasionally so that they cook evenly.

In a frying pan, heat ½ cup salad oil. Drain some of the beans, saving the liquid, and add them to the hot oil and mash completely. This serves to thicken the beans into a gravy. Add more reserved liquid a bit at a time, and more of the drained beans, until all the liquid has been used. Then continue cooking, stirring frequently until the mixture is of the thickness desired. The stirring is important as the beans burn easily. Serves 4 to 6.

FRUIT BASKET

Serve an arrangement of tropical fruits such as guavas, bananas, papayas, pineapple, oranges, and any melons in season. The pineapple can be cored, peeled and sliced, but put back together to look uncut. The other fruits are easy to eat with little or no preparation.

MOROCCO

An Elegant Buffet (Supper Menu)

(Cold dishes deliciously flavored, beautifully decorated,
and made mostly the day before)

Hors-D'oeuvres
Viennese Eggs with Swiss Toast
Artichokes Parmesan
Green Pea Salad
Hot French Rolls
French Vanilla Ice Cream
or
Date Crunch Torte
Café

HORS-D'OEUVRES
Marinated Celery Root

1   large celery root
¾   cup olive oil
¼   cup tarragon vinegar
1   tablespoon pure honey
1   clove garlic, crushed
1   teaspoon salt
¼   teaspoon freshly grated pepper
½   teaspoon fresh paprika

Pare large celery root and cut into julienne strips. Cover with boiling water and cook only 1 minute. Drain. Combine the other ingredients to make a marinade and add the mixture to the celery root. Refrigerate for 24 hours before serving.

Arrange a large platter with sections for radishes cut in flowerettes, green stuffed olives, ripe olives, cherry tomatoes, wedges of honeydew melons with small lemon wedges in each, the celery root and cantaloupe balls. Arrange so that the colors of each are artful and appetizing. This platter, with the very French marinated celery root, sets the style for the Moroccan meal.

VIENNESE EGGS

1   dozen eggs
¾   cup dairy sour cream and mayonnaise mixed
1   can chopped ripe olives
    Salt
½   teaspoon dill weed
½   teaspoon onion powder

Prepare the day before: 1 dozen eggs (cook hard; cool and shell). Cut eggs in half lengthwise and gently remove yolks, taking care not to tear whites. Mash yolks to a paste with a fork, blend in dillweed, onion powder, ¾ cup sour cream mixed with mayonnaise and salt to taste. Spoon yolk mixture into whites, or use a pastry bag fitted with a rosette tip. Top each half egg with a quarter section of un-peeled lime and about ¼ tsp. chopped ripe olives. Cover the dish and chill until ready to serve. Serves 12.

SWISS TOAST

¼ lb. real Swiss Cheese
1 egg yolk
½ teaspoon salt
¼ teaspoon white pepper
½ teaspoon prepared white horseradish
⅓ cup light cream
10 slices pumpernickle bread

Finely shred ¼ lb. (1 cup) imported Swiss Cheese. Mix to a paste with 1 egg yolk, ½ tsp. salt, ¼ tsp. white pepper, ½ tsp. prepared horseradish and about ⅓ cup light cream. (If you wish, you can make this mixture several days ahead.) Cut off the crusts of 10 slices of heavy, coarse-textured pumpernickel bread and spread evenly with cheese mixture. Cut each slice in quarters. Arrange on baking sheet in single layer. Cover and chill. Bake in 375° oven for 8 to 10 minutes, or until cheese is melted. Serve immediately.

ARTICHOKES PARMESAN

2 cups (1 lb. each) artichoke bottoms
½ teaspoon minced chives
⅛ teaspoon pepper
3 packages (3-oz. each) cream cheese
Melted butter
Parmesan cheese, freshly grated

Drain two cups (1 lb. ea.) artichoke bottoms and rinse well in cold water. Pat dry. Into the hollow of each bottom sprinkle ½ tsp. minced chives and ⅛ tsp. pepper; fill with 3 pkgs. (3 oz. ea.) of softened cream cheese. Spread to smooth top even with rim of artichoke bottom. Dip bottoms in melted butter, and coat with grated Parmesan cheese. Bake uncovered in 375° oven for 12 to 15 minutes, or until heated through and Parmesan cheese is melted. Serve immediately. Serves 12.

GREEN PEA SALAD

6 10-oz. pkgs. frozen green peas
⅔ cup salad oil
⅓ cup red wine vinegar
1½ teaspoons salt
2 tablespoons minced fresh mint or crumbled dried mint leaves
1 cup finely chopped celery
½ cup dairy sour cream
Romaine or garden leaf lettuce
4 large peeled tomatoes

Cook 6 pkgs. (10 oz. ea.) frozen peas in a small amount of water until just heated through; they will still be firm. Drain and save ½ cup cooking liquid; to this add ⅔ cup salad oil, ⅓ cup red wine vinegar, the salt, and the crumbled dry or minced fresh mint. Pour over peas, cover and chill. This can be done early in the day. Just before serving, mix in 1 cup finely chopped celery and ½ cup commercial sour cream. Spoon onto a large lettuce-lined serving tray or bowl; border with skinned tomato wedges (this requires about four good-sized tomatoes). 12 to 14 servings.

FRENCH VANILLA ICE CREAM (see Index)

DATE CRUNCH TORTE

- 3 egg whites
- ½ teaspoon cream of tartar
- 1 teaspoon pure vanilla flavoring
- 20 soda crackers
- 1 cup granulated sugar
- 12 dates, chopped
- ½ to 1 cup chopped walnut meats
  Whipped cream, sweetened

Separate and beat the three egg whites until frothy, add cream of tartar and beat until stiff, then add in the vanilla flavoring.

Crush 20 soda crackers by pressing with hands or rolling pin, but don't crush them too fine. Mix with 1 cup granulated sugar. Fold in the beaten egg whites with the crackers, to mix thoroughly. Add walnuts and dates. Pour into a buttered 9-inch pie plate. Bake slowly in a 325° F. oven from 30 to 35 minutes. Cut in wedges and serve topped with sweetened heavy whipped cream, or you can use vanilla ice cream. Serves 6.

Tip: It is a good idea to put a few drops of lemon juice into a food chopper before grinding sticky fruits such as dates, raisins, figs, or nuts. The grinder will not only be easier to clean, but all the ingredients will be utilized rather than sticking to the grinder so much.

NETHERLANDS

Dinner Menu #1

Green Pea Soup
("Soup Purée Verts Pois")
Hardcooked Eggs with Caper Sauce
Fluffy Rice
Apple Meringue
("Apple Mit Merinque")
Tea

GREEN PEA SOUP
(Soup Pureé Verts Pois)

- 5 cups water
- 1 head of escarole
- 2 pounds shelled fresh peas, or 2 packages of frozen; thawed peas
- 1 large onion, chopped
- 1 stalk of celery, threaded, diced
- 1¼ teaspoon salt
- ¼ teaspoon freshly ground pepper
- 1 teaspoon sugar
- 2 tablespoons flour
- 2 cups light cream
- ⅛ teaspoon freshly ground nutmeg

Sauté the chopped onion and celery in butter until golden brown. In a large soup pot, put the escarole, peas and the sautéed onion and celery. In a large saucepan bring the water to a boil and pour over vegetables in the pot. Cover and cook over low heat for 20 minutes. Puree in an electric blender or force through a sieve, and return to pot the mashed vegetables. Mix flour and nutmeg with the cream and add to the soup, stirring steadily to the boiling point. Cook over lowered heat for another 5 minutes. Do not leave this while cooking; watch it carefully. Taste for any adjustment in seasoning.

HARDCOOKED EGGS WITH CAPER SAUCE

Cut hardcooked eggs in half and pour the following sauce over them:

- 1 cup mayonnaise
- 4 tablespoons drained capers (purchased in jars)
- 4 tablespoons minced parsley
- 2 teaspoons vinegar from Capers

Gradually add the two teaspoons of vinegar into the mayonnaise and add other ingredients. Makes about 1½ cups of sauce.

Capers are pickled flower buds from a low shrub (*Capparis Spinosa*) of Mediterranean countries and used as a condiment. They are excellent in salads, sauces and with vegetables. They come in jars sold in gourmet sections of your grocery or market.

FLUFFY RICE

Prepare rice according to package instructions. Serve as a vegetable with butter rather than with sugar and cream.

APPLE MERINGUE (Apple Mit Meringue)

An unpretentious but very pleasant and easy dessert.

2 pounds green apples; must be tart, peeled, cored
¼ cup melted butter
⅓ cup yellow raisins, plumped
⅔ cup sugar
2 tablespoons fresh lemon juice
3 egg whites
½ teaspoon salt

Cut apples into ¼ inch slices. Place in a well-buttered shallow baking dish. Pour melted butter over apples. Sprinkle with raisins, lemon juice and half of the sugar. Cover with foil.

Bake in a preheated oven 350° F. for 20 minutes or until apples are tender but still shapely. Beat the egg whites with salt until stiff. Gradually beat in the remaining sugar to make stiff meringue. Spread meringue over the apples to the edge of the dish. Bake for an additional 10 minutes or until the meringue is golden brown. Serve warm with heavy cream, if desired.

Dinner Menu #2

Cheese Croquettes
(Croquettes au fromage)
Stewed Tomatoes
Homemade Amsterdam Green Bean Salad
(Gruner Bohnensalat)
Chocolate Mousse (Mousse au Chocolat)
Café

CHEESE CROQUETTES (makes 18)

- 4 tablespoons butter
- 7 tablespoons flour
- 1¾ cups milk
- ½ pound Swiss Cheese, grated
  Salt and pepper to taste
  Butter for sautéeing
- 1 egg, plus 3 yolks (beaten)
- 1 tablespoon oil
  Flour
  Dry bread crumbs

Melt butter over low heat, add 6 tablespoons of the flour and stir until golden color. Add 1½ cups milk and stir until thick and smooth. Cook slowly for about 10 minutes, stirring constantly. Season with salt and pepper. Remove from heat. Add the grated cheese and stir until melted. Add 3 egg yolks and stir. Spread evenly into a well-buttered shallow dish about 6 by 9 inches. Let cool then cover with wax paper and chill for about 2 hours. Cut into 18 or 20 pieces and shape into croquettes.

Now beat the whole egg with the remaining tablespoon of flour, the remaining portions of milk and the oil. Roll each croquette in flour then dip in the egg mixture, drain well on wax paper and then roll in fine bread crumbs. Chill for about 30 minutes. Sauté in butter over medium fire until golden brown on all sides, or they may be deep fried in oil, but the oil should not be too hot or the croquettes will split open. Can be served with Hollandaise, Bernaise, Caper Sauce or your favorite sauce, such as a tomato sauce if other tomatoes are not served with the meal. The recipe for Caper Sauce is with the previous menu.

STEWED TOMATOES

- 1 can tomatoes
- 1 teaspoon salt
- 2 pieces buttered toast
- 4 tablespoons butter
- 2 tablespoons sugar
  Dash of pepper

If using canned tomatoes with peels, try to remove the larger pieces of peelings and cut tomatoes into 6 or 8 smaller bite-size pieces. Pour tomatoes in their juice, with salt and sugar into a small sauce pan and heat until sugar is melted and no longer grainy. Butter a loaf pan or small casserole dish well. Butter well two slices of bread and toast on one side only in the broiler so that it remains buttery in the middle and browned on the edges only. When the tomatoes have cooked down a bit and there is not so much liquid, pour into the casserole. Slice each piece of toast into three strips and place across the top of the tomatoes. Sprinkle a dash of fresh ground pepper on the top and dot with butter. Place in oven at 350° F. for 12 or 15 minutes and serve.

AMSTERDAM GREEN BEAN SALAD

1½ lbs. green beans
Boiling salted water
¼ cup olive oil
2-3 tablespoons vinegar, or more to taste
Salt and pepper
1 teaspoon prepared mustard
1 onion, minced or thinly sliced
2 tablespoons parsley
1 teaspoon dried tarragon, or chervil, or 1 tablespoon fresh of either (optional)

Cook the beans in boiling water until tender, but still crisp. Make a dressing with the oil, vinegar, salt, pepper, mustard, onion and parsley. Drain the beans and put them in a bowl. While they are still hot, toss with the dressing. (If the beans are allowed to cool, the salad will not be as flavorful.) Add the herbs and allow to stand at room temperature for two hours. Do not chill.

CHOCOLATE MOUSSE
(Mousse au Chocolat)

Mousse au chocolat is one of the most delightful classic desserts of the French chef's repertoire. Make it one day ahead. It keeps well for several days when refrigerated. It is included in this menu since the Dutch are justly famous for their chocolate.

2 cups dark Dutch chocolate
5 egg yolks, beaten
½ cup strong black coffee
6 egg whites, beaten stiff
¼ teaspoon salt
¾ cup sugar
2 tablespoons rum extract (a flavoring)
1 teaspoon pure vanilla

Melt the chocolate in the top of a double boiler over hot, boiling water. Stir occasionally until the chocolate is softened. Add the beaten egg yolks, stir well to blend and cook for another 2 minutes. Remove from the heat and allow to cool while the egg whites are beaten. Add salt to the egg whites and gradually beat in the sugar, about 2 tablespoons at a time, until the mixture is glossy.

Fold in the chocolate mixture and add the rum and vanilla flavorings. Pile lightly into 6 small individual soufflé ramekins (pots de creme). Chill for 8 hours or overnight. Serve with whipped cream sweetened to taste. Serves 6 elegantly.

Supper Menu
Asparagus Au Gratin
Heated Slices of French Bread
with Garlic Butter
Chicory Salad
(Tea or Coffee)

ASPARAGUS AU GRATIN

1   or 2 bunches of fresh asparagus (2 lbs. serves 4)
4   hardboiled eggs (add 1 egg per guest)
2   tablespoons butter
2   tablespoons flour
2   tablespoons milk
1   cupful soft bread crumbs
¾   cup grated Swiss cheese or freshly grated Parmesan
1   teaspoon grated onion
½   cup of dried, buttered crumbs
     Salt and pepper to taste

Cut the asparagus, after washing, into 1 inch pieces and boil or steam until tender. Boil, shell and slice the eggs. Make a cream sauce with butter, flour and milk. Cover the bottom of the shallow casserole with thin layer of the sauce to which you added the bread crumbs, salt and white pepper. Make certain to butter the casserole well before adding the sauce. Drain asparagus which has been steamed or boiled and add a layer to baking dish au gratin which you cover with a layer of the sliced egg; repeat until the dish is filled — a layer of the sauce with bread crumbs, a layer of asparagus, a layer of sliced egg. Sprinkle the top with grated cheese and buttered bread crumbs. Bake in a hot oven, 400° F., until the food is hot and the crumbs are brown (10 to 20 minutes). Watch carefully. If you have any left over, heat in a double boiler, adding milk to thin it to desired consistency and also you will have an equally delicious soup. If you don't eat cheese, use ½ cup chopped olives instead. You can omit onion.

FRENCH BREAD buttered, with a little garlic powder (if you and your guest like it), and heated while the au gratin dish is finishing. Slice in ¾ inch slices but not all the way through the bottom crust. Garlic butter between each slice and tie a string lengthwise around loaf loosely while you heat in oven for the butter to melt and run down. Serve whole, letting guests pull off hot slices for themselves.

SALAD MIXED AT THE TABLE

    Chicory, or other fresh greens
3 firm ripe tomatoes
½ head of fresh white cauliflower
1 bunch green scallions
    Salad oil
    Vinegar
    Salt
    Pepper
    Herbs

The salad mainly consists of shredded chicory, small wedges of tomato, wafer-thin slices of raw cauliflower, slices of tiny scallions. Have ready a tray with salad oil, vinegar, salt, pepper in grinder. Make certain your greens are perfectly dry. There should not be a pool in the bottom of the bowl. Salad greens should be washed before being put in refrigerator to crisp. If you like, a few sprigs of fresh herbs: parsley, sweet basil, thyme, marjoram, or tarragon may be added. This is the joy of having a friend with an herb garden.

NEW ZEALAND

Homemade Tomato Soup
Nut Roast
Buttered Green Beans with Diced Carrots
New Zealand Salad
Crescent Rolls
Easy Cheese Cake or
Kiwi Fruit and selection of Cheeses

HOMEMADE TOMATO SOUP

1½ pounds tomatoes, cut in halves
2   large stalks celery, chopped finely
2   medium onions, chopped
1   large grated carrot
½   teaspoon each of sweet basil, thyme,
     garlic salt, salt
¼   teaspoon pepper
2   pints (4 cups) stock made with vegetarian
     bouillon
1¼ tablespoons flour, or 1 cubed potato
     Sugar
     Butter or salad oil

Peel and chop the onions; wash and chop celery; sauté gently in butter for about five minutes. Do not brown. Stir in the stock, herbs, tomatoes and potato with the onion and celery mixture. Simmer for about 30 minutes, until all vegetables are tender. Some prefer to take out the vegetables and press thru a sieve and return them to the pot. Add sugar, and additional salt and pepper to taste.

NUT ROAST

1   cup walnuts
1   cup cashew nuts
1   cup blanched almonds
1   cup bread crumbs
1   cup cooked brown rice
1   cup tomato purée
1   cup grated celery
¼   cup wholemeal flour
¼   cup gluten flour
2   tablespoons salad oil
2   large onions, chopped
2   eggs
1   teaspoon kelp granules
1   teaspoon vegetarian paste or liquid
     bouillon stock
2   tablespoons brewer's yeast
2   teaspoons soy sauce
1   teaspoon sea salt
3   teaspoons each of rosemary,
     basil, thyme, and minced parsley

Sauté onion and celery for about 5 minutes in salad oil; do not brown. Put all nuts, rice, and bread crumbs in food grinder, then add the flour, kelp, seasonings and herbs to the mixture. Place the tomato purée in a separate bowl and to it add the dissolved vegetarian bouillon, soy sauce, yeast and when mixed combine with the nut-crumb mixture. Last, fold in the slightly beaten eggs. Place in well-buttered baking dish, preferably a loaf pan shape, and dot top with butter. Bake in oven heated to 350°F. for 45 minutes.

BUTTERED GREEN BEANS WITH DICED CARROTS

2 packages of frozen, diagonally-cut green beans
1 package of frozen diced carrots
  Butter

Prepare vegetables according to package instructions, adding salt to the water. If cooked in salted water, vegetables require less salt and the taste cooks into them. Drain well, and add butter.

NEW ZEALAND SALAD

1 head lettuce, small
1 carrot, grated
½ green pepper, seeded and chopped
1 small cucumber, peeled, sliced thin
1 handful parsley, chopped
1 pint dandelion leaves
¼ head cabbage, finely chopped
2 stalks of celery, threaded, thin sliced
1 large apple, peeled and chopped
½ cup raisins

4 mint leaves, chopped fine

Wash vegetables but do not soak. Dry and chill in refrigerator in plastic bag. Just before serving, grate and chop as called for, otherwise there is a loss of necessary vitamins if done too far in advance.

Dressing:

1 cup olive oil
⅓ cup cider vinegar
1 teaspoon kelp granules
2 teaspoons soy sauce

Mix in small jar or cruet with tight top and shake to blend just before using. Pour over mixed salad greens and toss. Serve immediately.

CRESCENT ROLLS

1 cake or package of yeast
¼ cup lukewarm water
¾ cup milk
½ cup butter (not margarine)
4 tablespoons sugar
1 teaspoon salt
3 eggs, beaten
4½ cups sifted flour

In a bowl, drop yeast in the water. When milk is scalded add butter, sugar and salt. Allow to become lukewarm and stir in yeast, eggs and flour. Knead until smooth dough is formed. Place in greased bowl and cover. Allow to rise until bulk is doubled. Divide dough in thirds and roll each piece into a 10-inch circle. Cut into 12 wedge-shaped pieces. Roll up each piece from the wide end to the point. Place on a greased baking pan and pull ends inward to make a crescent. When it has risen again to double in bulk, brush with melted butter. Bake in a 400°F. oven for 15 minutes or until browned.

EASY CHEESE CAKE

3 packages (8-oz. each) cream cheese
4 eggs, beaten
1 pint commercial sour cream
1 cup sugar
½ tablespoon vanilla extract
16 Graham crackers
  Butter

Let cream cheese soften to room temperature. Add beaten eggs and stir thoroughly. Add the remaining ingredients and beat until smooth. Butter a low square baking pan and fill bottom with finely crushed Graham crackers and pack down; you may add a little melted butter to the crackers if you choose. Pour batter into pan, then set the baking pan into a larger pan with ¼-inch of water. Bake in 400°F. oven for 1 hour. Cool before serving. Serves 9.

PHILIPPINES

A Filipino Party Luncheon
Luscious Fruit Plate w/Chantilly Dressing
Stuffed Tomato Salad (In Saladang Camatis)
Malayasian Chicken (meatless)
Hot Rolls
Coffee
French Vanilla Ice Cream

CHANTILLY DRESSING

1 large package cream cheese
3 tablespoons cream
   Juice of 1 lemon
¼ teaspoon salt
2 tablespoons tart currant jelly
1 teaspoon chopped candied ginger, or
   more if desired
3 tablespoons whipped cream

Soften cream cheese to room temperature and thin by mixing with cream. Add the juice of 1 lemon, the salt and a bit of finely chopped candied ginger. If you have no currant jelly, tart plum jelly can be used or this ingredient can be omitted entirely. Add whipped cream last and chill thoroughly before serving in a glass bowl allowing guests to help themselves in the amount they want on their Fruit Plate.

LUSCIOUS TROPICAL FRUITS

Combination #1
   Lettuce
   Mangoes
   Papayas
   Cottage Cheese
   Strawberries

Arrange on individual plates: Garden lettuce, quartered; peeled, washed and ripened mangos; halves of papaya. Do not cut before serving. Both fruits should be ripened until firmly soft. A scoop of cottage cheese gives protein, is attractive and no other dressing is necessary. If it is the season, 2 or 3 strawberries gives an interesting color note.

Combination #2:

½ Mango for each guest
½ Avocado for each guest
4 ripe, red cherry tomatoes, or
4 or 5 grapes
   Young dandelion greens or the inner small leaves of lettuce
   Cold pressed olive oil
   Blanched almonds

For each serving: A half of small mango sliced, indescribably delicious. Half of a soft-to-touch avocado peeled, seeded, and sliced thick. Four firm, bright red, cherry tomatoes or either one of three varities of grapes, Concord, Catawba, and Salem. Cut grapes in halves and remove seeds. (The grape is truly a wonderful boon to mankind. Its praises have been sung by poets from time immemorial and few foods are nutritionally more rewarding.) One cleaned scallion finely chopped, tender dandelion greens or small leaves of lettuce centers arranged on individual plates. Pass cold pressed olive oil for dressing. Have fresh lemon quarters for those who want it. In tiny Oriental leaf dishes pass blanched almonds.

Combination #3:

1   Bartlett or Seckel pear per serving
    Fresh or canned or preserved figs
    Seedless grapes

Bartlett or Seckel pears (unlike some other fruits, pears attain a fine flavor when rippened off the tree). Preserved figs and grapes, seedless on a bed of crisp lettuce. Serve with Chantilly dressing.

Combination #4:

1   Persian melon
1   Cranshaw melon
2   tablespoons lime juice
2   tablespoons honey
¼   teaspoon each of ground coriander and nutmeg
    Choice of other fruits

1 each medium sized Cranshaw melon and medium sized Persian melon, 2 tablespoons lime juice (1 large lime), 2 tablespoons honey, ¼ teaspoon each ground corinander and nut-

meg. Cut melons in halves, remove and discard seeds. Cut fruit into balls of different sizes, using melon (or French) ball cutter, or metal measuring spoons. Place fruit and all juices in a deep bowl. Mix together lime juice, honey, coriander, and nutmeg. Blend with the melon. Cover and chill. Spoon into serving bowls. Makes 8 to 10 servings. Serve any 3 varieties of the following — mangos, papaya, fresh figs, cherimoyas, sapodillas, soursops, sugar apples, sapotes.

Combination #5

2   oranges sliced
1   sweet grapefruit
    Pecans or nut butter

2 oranges sliced. Peel just before serving with 1 sweet grapefruit, shelled and unsalted, unroasted pecans. (For those who are unable to chew nuts, nut butter, made from fresh raw nuts can be used. Remember that nut butters made from roasted and salted nuts are made indigestible by the processing.) Finely ground and emulsified nuts have proven to be the very best substitutes for milk. Many children are sensitive to cow's milk and not infrequently mother's milk fails. Avoid overripe fruit. Wash rind prior to cutting and serving. Melons should comprise the entire meal.

Combination #6:

    Bananas
    Golden Delicious apple
    Dried figs
    Peach
    Lemon juice
    Black raspberries or bing cherries
    Whipped cream

In the Koran, the banana tree is referred to as the "Paradise Tree." Not only is it a most delicious fruit but a staple, obtainable at moderate cost and of high food value, which is easily digestible.

Arrange on separate individual plates a bed of lettuce or watercress. 1 banana sliced with lemon juice over it and a golden delicious apple with deep yellow color, peeled and seeded and cut in quarters. Dried black mission figs. 1 fresh Luscious peach, dipped in boiling water to peel and slice; black raspberries or bing cherries. Top with freshly whipped cream.

STUFFED TOMATO SALAD
(In Saladang Camatis)

6   medium tomatoes
1   can (1 lb. 4 oz.) pineapple tidbits
1   cup peanuts, coarsely chopped
2   tablespoons French dressing
    Chicory or curly endive

Peel 6 medium-sized tomatoes (see Tip #21) cut a thin slice from the top of each, then scoop out the inside with a teaspoon, being careful not to break the shell. Turn cups upside down on paper toweling to drain.

About 1 hour before serving combine 1 can (1 lb. 4 oz.) pineapple tidbits, drained with 1 cup coarsely chopped peanuts and 2 tablespoons French dressing in a medium salad bowl. Toss lightly to mix. Pile into tomato cups, chill.

When ready to serve, line each guest's plate with leaves of chicory or curly endive and top with a stuffed tomato. Serve with additional dressing. Serves 6.

MALAYSIAN CHICKEN (meatless)

2   medium-sized eggplants
¼   cup water
¼   teaspoon salt
½   cup salad oil
1   cup strong (triple strength) vegetarian broth
½   teaspoon coriander, ground
½   cup salted cashews, coarsely chopped
2   cups diced vegetarian chicken (soy protein)
2   stalks celery, diced
2   medium-sized onions, thinly sliced
2   teaspoons curry powder
2   tablespoons flour
1   tablespoon ginger, grated fresh
1½ teaspoon garlic salt
1   can (5 oz) water chestnuts, drained and thinly sliced
1   cup hot or cold cooked rice
2   tablespoons butter, melted
¼   cup fine dry bread crumbs

Cut eggplants in half, then scoop out the flesh, leaving the eggplant shells about ¼ inch thick. Set aside the shells. Cut the eggplant flesh in cubes and combine in a frying pan with water and salt. Cover and cook, stirring occasionally until water is absorbed. Then add ½ cup oil, celery, onions, and curry powder; blend and cook, stirring occasionally, over medium heat, until vegetables are soft, about 10 minutes. Blend in flour, and gradually add seasoning broth, ginger, garlic, salt, and coriander, and cook until thickened and bubbly.

Stir in water chestnuts, cashews, rice and chicken and heat until bubbly again, but do not boil as chicken made of soy protein would disintegrate. Keep mixture warm. Brush inside of eggplant shells with remaining 2 or 3 tablespoons oil; broil empty shells of eggplant 6 inches from heat until easy to pierce with a fork. Remove quickly from heat and pile mixture into shells. Melt butter and mix with bread crumbs, then drizzle over filled eggplant shells; brown very lightly under broiler. Watch carefully and do not leave too long.

FRENCH VANILLA ICE CREAM

4 egg yolks
2 cups milk
⅓ cup sugar
⅛ teaspoon salt
1 teaspoon pure vanilla extract
½ pint heavy cream, whipped

First make a custard as follows: Scald milk in double boiler. Put eggs in bowl and add sugar and salt; stir to mix thoroughly then pour scalded milk into the egg yolks and sugar, stirring constantly while adding. Wash out the boiler in which the milk was scalded, and then return the custard through a strainer into the top of the double boiler again. Keep water just below the boiling point, or custard will curdle. Now put the top boiler back in the double boiler and stir slowly until the custard thickens and becomes creamy. Remember it will not be as thick when hot as it will be when you chill it. The custard should be perfectly smooth and like fairly thin cream. In case the custard should curdle, remove the top boiler immediately and place it in cold water and beat the custard with a rotary egg beater. It will then become smooth again. Do not return to the fire, but chill. When custard is cold, add the vanilla and the ½ pint (1 cup) of heavy cream that has been whipped stiff, and freeze.

Using either the old-fashioned hand cranked freezer or one of the new electric ones, place the cooled mixture in the center container and pack in 3 parts ice to 1 part rock salt and turn until frozen. Makes 1½ quarts.

POLAND

Dinner Menu
Little Cold Summer Soup
(Chloduik)
Pastry Pockets
(Pierogi)
Fresh Green Peas and New Potatoes
Filled Turnip Cups
Salad Dish Marinade
Black Cherry Tart

POLISH COLD SUMMER SOUP
(Chloduik)

2½ quarts of water
 7 large beets, peeled and
     grated, save some tops
 3 beets, peeled and cubed
 1 large minced onion
 1 quart buttermilk
 6 hardcooked eggs
 2 cucumbers, sliced thin
 1 bunch radishes, sliced thin
2½ teaspoons dill weed
 2 cups dairy sour cream
     A few green beet tops or a little watercress

Put the 7 grated beets into 2½ quarts of salted boiling water and simmer with the onion over low heat for 1 hour. Slice very thinly the cucumbers and the radishes, mix in chopped hardboiled eggs and put into buttermilk. Peel, slice and cube the other three beets and set aside. When beets and onions have cooked, add the buttermilk mixture and the three cubed beets, so as to find chunks in the soup when served. Cook a bit longer and add watercress for only last minute of cooking. Add the dill weed to the sour cream and let sit. When soup is cooled, serve with a dollop of sour cream on top of each bowl.

PIEROGI
(Pastry Pockets)

 2 cups sifted flour
 ½ teaspoon salt
 ¾ cup butter (not margarine)
 1 egg yolk
 4 tablespoons ice water

Sift flour and salt. Work in the butter with blender. Beat the egg yolk and water together and add to the flour mixture. Toss lightly and form into a ball.

Roll out the dough ⅛ inch thick and cut into 3-inch circles. Use one tablespoon of each of the following fillings for each. Chill. Fold pastry over into a half-moon and press the edges together with a little water. Arrange on a greased baking sheet.

Bake in a 400° F. oven for 15 minutes or until browned. Makes about 24.

Fillings:

#1 Eggplant

1 eggplant (1 lb.) cubed
1 medium onion, chopped fine
1 pound fresh mushrooms
2 yolks of hardcooked eggs
3 tablespoons sour cream
4 tablespoons bread crumbs
1½ teaspoons salt
  Dash of cayenne pepper

Use butter or shortening (not oil) to sauté eggplant. Separately, sauté the onion, then mix with eggplant. Clean the mushrooms and slice. Sauté in 3 tablespoons butter for 15 minutes. Chop the mshrooms with the egg yolks and mix with eggplant and onion. Stir in 3 tablespoons sour cream, the bread crumbs and the seasonings. Fill pockets with mixture and bake.

#2 Mushroom ("Uszki" Pelmeni)

1 1 pound mushrooms, sliced
¾ cup minced onions
3 tablespoons butter
2 hardcooked egg yolks
3 tablespoons sour cream
3 tablespoons bread crumbs
1½ teaspoons salt
  Dash cayenne pepper

Cook the mushrooms and the onions in the butter for 15 minutes. Chop the mushroom mixture and egg yolks together. Stir in the sour cream, pepper and bread crumbs. Fill into Pierogi pastry pockets for baking.

#3 Cheese

½ pound pot cheese (or cottage cheese)
¼ pound cream cheese
1 egg yolk
1 teaspoon salt
1 tablespoon sugar (optional)

Beat ingredients together. Sugar is optional depending on whether or not you like a sweet filling. Fill pockets and bake. Serve with sour cream.

#4 Cabbage

Cabbage requires a different dough mixture. Recipes for the dough and the filling follows:

Bread Dough for Cabbage Pieroski

2½ cups sifted flour
1 teaspoon baking powder
½ teaspoon salt
2 eggs
⅔ cup salad oil
2 tablespoons water

Sift the flour, baking powder and salt into a bowl. Make a well in the center and drop the eggs, oil and water into it. Work these into the flour with the hands and knead until smooth. Divide the dough into two parts. Roll out as thin as possible. Brush with oil. Now cut the rolled dough into 3-inch circles and place a tablespoon of the cabbage filling on each. Draw in the edges and pinch them firmly together. Place on an oiled baking sheet the pinched side up. Bake in an oven heated to 375° for 35 minutes or until browned. Makes about 24.

Filling: Cabbage Pieroski:

½ head cabbage, cooked and chopped
¾ cup minced onions
3 hardcooked egg yolks
3 tablespoons honey
¼ cup lemon juice
¼ cup raisins
1 tablespoon potato flour
Salt and pepper to taste

Mix ingredients together to make the center filling. Place 1 tablespoon of this savoury on each dough circle.

or

If you do not care for a sweet pieroski, just steam a young cabbage you have quartered and cored, for about 10 minutes. It is good to somewhat separate the leaves before steaming so that the inner leaves will cook also. Drain and chop fine. Finely chop 2 sweet white onions and sauté in butter but do not let brown. Mash the egg yolks and mix with the finely chopped cabbage and the sautéed onions. Add salt and pepper to taste. Fill the pastry round and pinch together. These can be baked, fried or boiled. Serve with a dollop of sour cream.

Filling #5 Prune:

¼ cup pure honey
¾ cup orange juice
2 tablespoons lemon juice
1 pound unsweetened, pitted prunes
1 tablespoon grated orange rind

Cook honey, orange juice and lemon juice for 5 minutes. Add the prunes and cook over low heat for 15 minutes, stirring occasionally.

Drain and chop prunes. Add the orange peel. Cool before filling pastry pockets.

Filling #6
Entrée Pierogi — "Smazouy Ser" (Delicious cheese)

Slice thick, sharp cheddar cheese into the number of slices you want to serve. The slices should be approximately ⅜ of an inch in thickness.

Roll each slice in flour, then dip in beaten egg and roll in cracker crumbs or fine, crisp bread crumbs. Refrigerate for at least 1 hour. Sauté in butter, but do not use margarine. Serve hot.

FRESH GREEN PEAS AND NEW POTATOES

2½ to 3 pounds fresh peas
Salt
12 small red new potatoes
Butter

Shell peas into pan with salted water. If fresh garden peas are not available, use two packages of fresh frozen peas. Cook until tender but not so long that they lose their fresh green color. Separately, boil or steam the tiny new potatoes in their jackets. When tender, drain. Drain peas, add new potatoes to them and serve immediately in deep vegetable dish with lots of butter.

FILLED TURNIP CUPS

8   medium size turnips, washed and peeled
1   quart boiling water salted
1½ teaspoons salt
1   tablespoon butter
1   tablespoon minced onions
½   cup milk
⅛   teaspoon salt
    Paprika
    Bread or cracker crumbs

Drop the washed and peeled turnips in 1 quart of salted water already boiling. Cover and cook until tender. Remove turnips from water and hollow each of them, setting them in a shallow pan or baking dish with a few drops of water around them.

Chop the pulp removed from the center of turnips and sauté in 1 tablespoon of real butter for 3 minutes and combine with the minced onions. Season the turnip and onion mixture with salt and paprika and thicken slightly its consistency by adding cracker or bread crumbs. Fill the turnip cups with the mixture. Take the stuffed turnip cups from the water pan and place in a buttered baking dish. Combine milk and ⅛ teaspoon salt and pour over and around the turnip cups. Bake in an oven heated to 350° until slightly browned on top.

Turnips, both white and yellow, contain much natural potash, soda, lime and iron.

SALAD DISH MARINADE

2 or 3 small firm tomatoes
1 large cucumber
1 small sweet onion
  Water
  Vinegar
  Salt and pepper

Slice tomatoes, peel and slice cucumbers, and slice onions separating into rings. Make a marinade of 2 parts of water to 1 part of vinegar, add salt and pepper. Place slices of three vegetables in deep dish to marinate in refrigerator. Drain most of liquid off before placing in dish for table, allow each guest to serve themselves.

BLACK CHERRY TART

1   pound can of black cherries
½   cup granulated sugar
½   cup cold water
1½ tablespoons cornstarch
1   cup whipping cream, beaten until stiff.

Strain juice from can of cherries into a small pan; add sugar. In ½ cup of cold water, dissolve the cornstarch and add this to the cherry juice. Bring liquid to a boil and allow to simmer very slowly for 30 minutes. Split the cherries in half and remove the stones. Place cherries in bowl and pour the heavy, thickened juice syrup from the pan over them and chill.

Bake a pastry shell (see Index for recipe)

To combine whip the cream until stiff and fill the baked pastry shell with whipped cream. Pour the cold cherries with the heavy syrup over the cream and serve.

PORTUGAL

Supper Menu
Portuguese Eggs
Parsleyed Potatoes
Lemon Butter Squash
Celery Hearts and Olives
Pot de Creme Au Chocolat
Demi Tasse

PORTUGUESE EGGS

6   hardcooked
2   tablespoons butter
1   onion, finely minced
4   tomatoes, cut in pieces
1   small can mushrooms
1   teaspoon grated lemon peel
2   heaping tablespoons flour
2   cups milk
½   teaspoon salt
¼   teaspoon pepper
1   heaping tablespoon minced parsley
1   tablespoon lemon juice

Make a white sauce with melted butter and flour in a small saucepan, and stirring constantly add the milk and cook until the sauce thickens. Give it a total of 10 minutes cooking time to rid it of the starchy taste. Add salt, pepper, parsley, lemon juice and rind. Cut hardcooked eggs into quarters and arrange in a shallow dish.

In a small skillet sauté the onion and add mushrooms to slightly brown. Remove onions and mushrooms then put cut up tomatoes in skillet for a brief sautéing. Add onions, mushrooms and tomatoes to the white sauce and pour over eggs in a shallow dish. Asparagus and other green vegetables in season are colorful served with this platter. Makes 6 servings.

PARSLEYED POTATOES

6   medium size potatoes, peeled and halved
4   sprigs of fresh parsley, minced fine
4   tablespoons butter

Peel and halve the potatoes and put in cold, salted water to boil. Cook, covered until tender. In a small saucepan, melt the butter and add the finely minced parsley to it. Drain potatoes completely then pour parsleyed butter over them in serving dish.

LEMON BUTTER SQUASH

4   or 5 small fresh yellow summer squash
2   teaspoons salt
2   or 3 tablespoons lemon juice
2   tablespoons butter
    Artificial butter flavor, a few drops

Clean and thinly slice squash in rounds. Place in salted water with 1 or 2 tablespoons lemon juice and 2 tablespoons butter. Let boil rapidly for 15 minutes. Add more lemon juice just before they are cooked and a drop or two of butter flavoring. Drain, place in bowl and top with butter and serve immediately.

CELERY HEARTS AND OLIVES

Arrange an attractive relish tray by alternating slender celery hearts, green pimento-stuffed olives, ripe olives alternately. One can also add small carrot sticks and radish roses for color. This fresh crispy tray is in place of a salad.

POT DE CREME AU CHOCOLAT

3   egg yolks
¼   cup sugar
1   cup light cream, heated
1   6-oz. package semi-sweet chocolate
    pieces
1   teaspoon vanilla
    Sweetened whipped cream

In a small bowl of an electric mixer, beat the egg yolks at high speed. Gradually add sugar and continue to beat until mixture is thick and lemon colored. Reduce speed to low and gradually add light cream. Turn mixture into a saucepan, place over low heat and cook, stirring constantly until mixture is slightly thickened—about 5 to 8 minutes. Remove from heat and add chocolate and vanilla, stirring until chocolate is melted. Pour mix into ramekins or into demitasse cups. Makes six. Chill several hours until set.
Garnish with sweetened whipped cream.

RUSSIA

Hearty Winter Dinner
Borscht
Ukrainian Egg Rissoles
Rice-Stuffed Cabbage
Creamed Onions
Pickled Beets and Onion Rings
Turnip Salad
Quick Kulich with Lemon Glaze
Hot Spiced tea

RUSSIAN COLD BORSCHT

10 large beets, peeled and grated
2½ quarts water
1 large onion, minced
2 teaspoons salt
3 tablespoons brown sugar
¼ cup lemon juice (juice of 2 lemons)
2 eggs
1 cup commercial sour cream

Combine the beets, water, minced onion and salt in a large saucepan. Bring to a boil and cook over lowered heat, simmering for 1 hour. Add sugar and lemon juice. Cook another 10 minutes and taste to correct and adjust seasonings.

Beat the eggs in a bowl. Gradually add the soup, stirring steadily to prevent curdling. Chill soup and serve with hot boiled potatoes. Garnish with sour cream. Makes about 2 quarts.

UKRAINIAN EGG RISSOLES

4 tablespoons butter
1 tablespoon cornflour
1 cup milk
2 tablespoons grated cheese
¼ teaspoon mace or nutmeg
  Salt and pepper to taste
4 eggs, hardcooked
2 tablespoons fresh parsley, minced
  Flour for coating
  Cooking oil

Melt butter in pan and blend in the cornflour. Remove from heat and gradually add the milk, stirring. Bring to a boil until mixture thickens. It should be a stiff mixture. Add the seasonings and grated cheese and allow to melt before adding the well-chopped hardcooked eggs, and add parsley last. When mixture has cooled a little, shape into rissoles (like rounded patties) coat with flour and sauté on both sides in very hot salad oil until golden brown. These are often served with grilled tomatoes and fresh green or snap beans.

RICE-STUFFED CABBAGE

1 head cabbage
2 eggs
4 tablespoons grated onion
2 cups half-cooked rice
1½ cups seedless raisins
2 teaspoons salt
4 tablespoons butter
2 white onions, sliced
1 tablespoon potato flour
2 cups boiling water
2 tablespoons lemon juice
2 teaspoons sugar
½ teaspoon cinnamon
½ cup dairy sour cream

Put head of cabbage into deep pan and pour boiling water over it and let stand for 10 minutes. Remove top 18 leaves, but if they are not large enough, use 24 leaves.

Beat the eggs and gradually add the grated onion, rice, salt, and half the raisins. Place a heaping tablespoon of this mixture on each cabbage leaf and carefully roll up.

Melt butter in a casserole. Lightly brown the onions and the cabbage rolls in it. Sprinkle them with the potato flour, and the boiling water with lemon juice, sugar, cinnamon and the remaining salt and raisins. Bake in oven at 350° for an hour and 15 minutes, basting frequently. Stir in the sour cream just before seving. This recipe serves 6 to 8.

QUICK CREAMED ONIONS

1 pound frozen small white onions
  (half a large frozen bag)
2 cans cream of mushroom soup
1 cup milk
⅛ teaspoon thyme
  Salt to taste, as canned soup is salty
½ cup slivered almonds

Cook small white onions until tender, but do not allow to break. If preferred, you can use canned onions, but drain and rinse first. Heat the two cans of mushroom soup thinned slightly with the milk. Add thyme. Place onions in buttered casserole and pour soup over them. Top with almonds. Bake slowly in oven heated to 350°, covered. The onions should be tender. Serves 6 to 8.

PICKLED BEETS AND ONION RINGS

1 small can sliced beets
1 small sweet onion, peeled
  and sliced thin.
1 tablespoon or less of vinegar

Add vinegar to juice of canned beets. Separate raw white onion rings and mix with beet slices, to marinate. Serve as a side dish.

TURNIP SALAD

Choose tender, young turnips. Peel thinly and grate on fine grater. Dress with fresh squeezed lemon juice and season with salt and pepper. Though it doesn't often suit the American taste, this is often made with vinegar in Europe rather than the lemon juice. The addition of finely chopped apple also gives it a delicious taste.

QUICK KULICH
(Makes 1 large or 2 medium breads)

1 package of hot roll mix
¼ cup very warm water
3 eggs at room temperature
¼ cup sugar
⅛ teaspoon saffron threads
3 tablespoons soft butter,
⅓ cup light or dark raisins
⅓ cup candied red cherries
   (halved)
⅓ *cup slivered toasted almonds*

Sprinkle yeast from the hot roll mix into the warm water in a large bowl. Stir until yeast dissolves. Add eggs, sugar and saffron threads; beat well until blended. Beat in about ½ of the roll mix until smooth. With electric mixer set at medium speed, beat in the butter until it is absorbed into the dough. Stir in the remaining roll mix with a spoon, to let rise in a warm place, away from any draft, for 1 to 1½ hours, or until doubled in bulk.

Meanwhile, pour flavoring over the raisins and cherries in a small bowl and let stand to soak, stirring often, wile the dough rises.

Stir dough down, then add fruit mixture and almonds. Stir until evenly spread throughout dough. Grease well a 3-lb. shortening can or two 1-pound coffee cans and turn the dough into these. Cover with a towel and again let rise for an hour or hour and a half until doubled again in bulk. Bake in moderate oven, heated to 350°, for 40 minutes or until bread is richly brown on top and gives a hollow sound when tapped. Turn out onto plate and let it cool. Pour lemon glaze over top, letting it dribble down the sides of the bread. Decorate with fruits and nuts if you wish. To serve, cut off the top of the Kulich, then cut as many round slices as needed. Replace top to prevent bread from drying. Halve slices and arrange around base of the bread on platter.

LEMON GLAZE

Combine ½ cup 10X confectioner's sugar and 1 tablespoon lemon juice in a small cup. Stir with spoon until smooth and pour over Kulich.

HOT SPICED RUSSIAN TEA

1 teaspoon whole cloves
1 inch stick cinnamon
6 cups cold water
6 to 8 black tea bags
¾ cup fresh orange juice
2 tablespoons lemon juice
½ cup granulated sugar

Add spices to water, bring to a rolling boil. Add tea, cover and let steep for 5 minutes. Strain tea into a samovar—a copper or brass urn for heating water to make tea. The hostess serves the tea from the samovar, a typical Russian urn. You may strain the tea into a heated teapot or carafe. Heat juices and sugar to boiling and add to hot tea. Makes 6 to 8 servings.

SPAIN

Spanish Luncheon
Gazpacho
Eggs Espagnol
Chicory Boats Cucumber Salad
Spanish Custard Flan
Coffee

GAZPACHO

There are two versions of gazpacho — the Spanish cold tomato soup. To be typically Spanish, the vegetables are chopped and combined with the seasoned tomato juice. Bread sticks are the usual accompaniment.

In Mexico one is more likely to find that part of the vegetables have been puréed with the tomato juice. The rest are then served, chopped, to be added as desired along with garlic croutons. Either way, the results are refreshing and most delicious.

Spanish version:

3 large tomatoes, peeled and chopped
1 bunch green onions, minced
1 green pepper, chopped
1 cucumber, chopped (and peeled if waxed)
2½ cups tomato juice
⅓ cup wine vinegar
¼ cup olive oil
1 teaspoon salt
1 clove garlic, mashed

½ teaspoon fresh ground pepper
⅛ teaspoon Tabasco sauce

Prepare all the vegetables. Combine the tomato juice with remaining ingredients. Stir in the vegetables and chill for several hours to allow the tastes to blend. Makes 1½ quarts.

Mexican version:

2 large tomatoes, peeled and chopped fine
1 medium onion, chopped fine
½ green pepper
½ large cucumber

This version differs only that you save aside a small portion of the finely chopped vegetables to serve as condiments for guests to select, these are on a divided serving dish or in small individual bowls.

EGGS ESPAGNOL (Entrée)

2 jars (10-oz. each) artichoke hearts
⅓ cup chopped onion
⅓ cup chopped green pepper
1 clove garlic, pressed

2 tablespoons butter or olive oil
2 cans (8 oz. each) tomato sauce
2 tablespoons chopped fresh parsley
½ teaspoon each oregano and basil
1 teaspoon vinegar
½ teaspoon salt
Dash of pepper
12 hard-cooked eggs, shelled
¼ cup grated Parmesan cheese

Drain artichoke hearts. Sauté onion, green pepper, and garlic in olive oil or butter. Stir in tomato sauce, parsley, oregano, basil, vinegar, salt and pepper. Cut eggs in half lengthwise and arrange with artichokes in a shallow 9 x 13 inch baking dish. Spoon sauce over artichokes and eggs; top with cheese. Bake, uncovered, in a hot oven (425°F.) for 15 minutes, or until sauce is bubbly. Serve over steamed rice. Serves 6.

CHICORY BOATS

Fresh chicory
2 medium beets
French dressing
2 carrots
1 can Mandarin orange slices
Parsley

Wash and separate the chicory leaves, using the most attractive ones as boats. Grate finely the two cleaned carrots and the two scrubbed beets. Open can of mandarin orange slices and drain. Mix orange sections lightly with the carrots and beets. Pile into the Chicory boats and top with French dressing and garnish with a sprig of fresh parsley.

CUCUMBER SALAD

3 medium-sized cucumbers
1 teaspoon salt
3 tablespoons vinegar
1½ tablespoons olive oil
1 tablespoon parsley, minced
1 tablespoon green onion, minced
⅛ teaspoon black pepper
1 teaspoon dill weed

Wash cucumbers and peel thinly, if the skin is tough, or you can flute the skin by drawing the prongs of a fork down the length; slice into very thin rounds and sprinkle with salt. Allow to stand for an hour. Then drain liquid off cucumber. Sprinkle with 3 tablespoons vinegar, 1½ tablespoons olive oil, 1 tablespoon each parsley and green onion on top, ⅛ teaspoon black pepper and 1 teaspoon dill weed. Allow to marinate a half hour. Serve in a shallow glass dish. Each guest serves himself.

SPANISH CUSTARD FLAN Serves 6-8

(This dessert has a French cousin called caramel custard or "crème renversée au caramel")

¾ cup sugar
1 cup light cream
1½ cups milk
1 four-inch piece of stick cinnamon
4 eggs
2 teaspoons vanilla extract

1. Set oven to slow 325°F.; place an 8 x 8 x 1½-inch cake pan or a 4-5 cup ring mold in the oven to warm. (Caramelized sugar coats a warm mold more evenly).
2. Heat ⅓ cup of the sugar in a large skillet

over medium heat until sugar melts and turns golden. Remove pan or mold from oven; immediately pour caramelized sugar into pan. Hold pan with pot holder and tilt from side to side to cover bottom and sides of pan with the sugar.

3. Combine cream, milk, remaining sugar and the cinnamon in a medium-sized pan; heat just until bubbles form around edge.

4. Beat eggs slightly with vanilla in a medium-sized bowl; gradually pour in hot milk mixture, stirring constantly; strain into prepared pan. Place pan in large shallow pan; place on oven shelf; pour water into large pan to depth of only about ½ inch. (If too high the water in outside pan would spill over into the custard.) Be careful, if this happened it would spoil the custard.

5. Bake in slow oven 325°F. for 30 minutes, or until center is almost set. Remove from pan of water; cool, then chill several hours or overnight.

6. To unmold, loosen custard around edge with thin, small spatula. Cover pan with serving dish or plate; turn upside down, shaking gently to release custard; lift off mold. Spoon onto low glass dessert dishes with a little of the caramel syrup spooned over each serving. Garnish with whipped cream flavored with a little sugar and vanilla.

SWEDEN

Dinner Menu
Nut Croquettes
Swedish Pancakes w/ Mushroom Filling
Rutabaga Pie
Vegetable Salad
Swedish Rye Rolls
Swedish Nut Brittle Pudding
Special Swedish Coffee

NUT CROQUETTES

2½ cups ground walnut kernels
2 cups fine, dry bread crumbs
1 cup grated onion
1 carrot, ground raw
½ clove garlic crushed
1 green pepper, seeded
½ teaspoon salt
¼ teaspoon pepper
2 tablespoons minced parsley
4 eggs

In food chopper, grind together the nuts, bread, onions, green pepper, carrot and the garlic. Add the 2 beaten eggs and the seasonings. Mix well and shape into patties or croquettes. Beat the 2 remaining eggs and carefully dip the croquettes in it then rolling in fine cracker crumbs. Fry in hot vegetable oil until brown on all sides.

These may be pan fried or deep fried in vegetable oil. Peanut oil is preferable since it can be heated to a very high temperature without smoking.

SWEDISH PANCAKES

These thin pancakes have the texture of Swedish "plattar" and the shape of "crêpes". They are rolled with some of the mushroom filling inside and some over them.

½ cup flour
½ teaspoon sugar
¼ teaspoon salt
2 eggs, slightly beaten
1½ cups cream

Sift and measure the flour; re-sift flour with sugar and salt. Add the slightly beaten eggs and the cream. Beat with rotary beater until smooth. Using only 2 tablespoons at a time, sauté in a hot frying pan that is 6 inches in bottom diameter. Quickly tilt the pan so that the batter covers the bottom. Brown pancake about 1 minute on the first side, then with spatula turn it carefully to brown on the other side. Keep pancakes warm in a very slow oven while frying the remaining batter. Add more butter (do not substitute with margarine or other shortening) to the pan for each pancake. Roll each pancake up with 1 (one) tablespoon of the mushroom filling in each; place them side by side in a shallow buttered baking dish, approximately 7½" by 11 inches in size. Dot with butter, using as much as ¼ cup of butter; sprinkle with grated Gruyère cheese. Bake uncovered in a 425° oven for about 10 minutes, until cheese is melted. Serve with the remaining mushroom filling and sauce. Makes 12 filled pancakes. The same mushroom filling/sauce is also a fine sauce for a fluffly omelet.

MUSHROOM FILLING/SAUCE

½ pound fresh mushrooms, sliced
3 tablespoons each butter and flour
1 teaspoon salt
1½ cups light cream
1½ tablespoons lemon juice
¼ teaspoon pepper, or white pepper

Sauté mushroom slices in butter for about 5 minutes. Stir in the flour, salt and pepper. Add cream and cook, stirring constantly until thick and smooth. Stir in lemon juice. You will have about 2½ cups of this sauce.

RUTABAGA PIE (Lanttulaatikko)

2 pounds rutabagas (yellow turnips)
½ teaspoon salt
1½ cups fine dry bread crumbs
1 cup of light cream
  Dash ground white pepper
1 tablespoon sugar
⅛ teaspoon ground nutneg
2 eggs, lightly beaten
2 tablespoons butter

Peel rutabagas and cut into ½ inch cubes. Cook in just enough salted water to cover the cubes for about 30 minutes or until tender. Drain and mash. Stir in 1 cup of bread crumbs, 1 cup of light cream, sugar, pepper and nutmeg. Add more salt if needed. Stir in the lightly beaten eggs. Butter a round cake pan and coat it with bread crumbs. Fill pan with the turnip mixture and sprinkle the remaining crumbs on the top. Dot the top with butter and place in oven preheated to 325° for about an hour, until top is lightly browned. Serves 4.

VEGETABLE SALAD

1 cup cabbage, shredded fine
2 firm cooked beets, grated
2 carrots, coarsley grated
1 apple, peeled and grated
1 tablespoon lemon juice
½ cup mayonnaise
2 tablespoons milk

Combine cabbage, beets, carrots and apples. Immediately add lemon juice as it helps prevent the apples from turning brown. Blend the mayonnaise with the milk, add to vegetables and toss to mix well. Serves 4.

SWEDISH RYE ROLLS

4 cups unsifted white flour
2 cups unsifted rye flour
1 tablespoon salt
1 tablespoon caraway seeds
2 packages active dry yeast
2 cups water
⅓ cup dark molasses
½ cup butter (1 stick)
1 egg white, slightly beaten

In a large bowl thoroughly blend 2 cups of mixed flours with salt, caraway seeds and undissolved active dry yeast. Combine water, molasses and butter in a saucepan over low heat until the liquid warms, though butter does not need to melt. Gradually add the warm liquid to the dry ingredients and beat for 2 minutes at medium speed of electric mixer, scraping the bowl occasionally. Add ¾ cup of flour mixture, enough to make a thick batter. Beat at high speed for 2 minutes, remembering to scrape the bowl. Stir in enough additional flour mixture to make a soft dough. If necessary, you may add some additional white flour to make desired consistency. Turn dough out onto lightly floured board, knead until smooth and elastic, about 8 to 10 minutes. Place it in a greased bowl, turning it to grease top. Cover bowl and let dough rise in a warm place, free from draft, until doubled in bulk—about 45 minutes.

Punch dough down and turn out onto lightly floured board. Divide dough in half. Divide each half into 24 equal pieces. Form each piece into a ball. Grease 3 8-inch round cake pans and place 6 dough balls in each of the pans. Cover and let rise again in a warm place until again doubled in bulk; another 45 minutes.

Lightly brush the tops with slightly beaten egg white and sprinkle with caraway seeds. Bake in oven preheated to 350° for 20- to 25 minutes, or until done. These rye rolls make a delicious, pungent dinner roll, nice with any meal. Repeat the last steps with the other half of the dough, making it into 24 balls, etc..

Rye grains are grown and flourish in damp cool climates so it grows profusely in the Scandanavian countries. The crisp, flat, crackerlike rye breads imported from northern Europe are familiar around the world. Originally they were made during the years when weather conditions shortened the growing season. The immature grain had to be harvested, baked and dried to prevent spoilage.

SWEDISH NUT BRITTLE PUDDING

1 envelope (1 tablespoon agar agar) gelatin
2 tablespoons cornstarch
4 tablespoons sugar
1¼ cups milk
3 eggs, separated
1 teaspoon vanilla
½ tablespoon rum extract
½ pint (1 cup) whipping cream
⅛ teaspoon salt
⅛ teaspoon cream of tartar
½ cup nut brittle

In the top of a double boiler, mix agar agar, cornstarch and 2 tablespoons sugar together. Stir in the milk. Beat egg yolks until light, and stir into mixture. Place over hot water and, stirring constantly, cook until thickened. Remove from heat and blend vanilla and rum flavoring. Chill until custard starts to set, then beat it until light and smooth. Whip the cream until stiff and fold it into the custard. Beat egg whites until foamy, then add salt and cream of tartar, then continue beating until stiff. Sprinkle remaining sugar and beat until stiff peaks form. Fold this meringue into the custard mixture.

Fold in ½ cup of crushed nut brittle. Turn into a 1½ quart serving dish or scoop into individual dishes and chill until firm. Garnish top with brittle.

NUT BRITTLE

1 cup sugar
¾ cup chopped filberts, almonds or peanuts

Place 1 cup sugar in frying pan and heat over low heat until sugar is melted and turns amber color. Add ¾ cup of chopped nuts and stir. Continue cooking until liquid sugar turns a caramel color. Turn out at once onto a buttered cookie sheet; let stand a few minutes to set. Then mark into 1-inch wide strips and mark across those lines diagonally to form diamond shapes. Let the candy cool. Crush ½ cup of this candy to sprinkle on Nut Brittle Pudding.

SWEDISH COFFEE

Famous everywhere for their always-ready pots of superb coffee, the Swedish have their own methods for making it.

Using a tall, enamelware pot they make their coffee nonetheless by the drip method by filtering it through a clean cloth. Simply buy a brand of Swedish coffee at a speciality import food shop or use your own brand. Boil water till it is bubbling briskly. Measure the coffee into a clean cloth and let it sag slightly into the enamelware coffeepot, pour the boiling water over the coffee and let it drip through the grounds in the cloth, filtering out any oily residue or bitterness. It can be kept hot or reheated in the large pot.

SWITZERLAND

Dinner Menu
Bisque Aux Champignons (Fresh Mushroom Bisque)
Spinatauflauf (Spinach Soufflé)
Kartoffelstock Mit Birnen (Country Mashed Potatoes with Pears)
La Scarpaza Di Blenio (Swiss Chard from the Val Di Blenio)
Chrisesibrägel (Cherry Pudding)   -   Coffee

Since Switzerland has three distinct languages among its population, the cuisine is naturally influenced by those countries—Germany, France and Italy. The menu above reflects each of the three. Yet Swiss Chocolate and Fondue are not among them. We thought you would like to become familiar with other Swiss cooking.

The addition of a fresh green salad, made with Bibb lettuce or watercress, with a fresh oil and vinegar dressing would top the meal off with just the right touch to this menu.

FRESH MUSHROOM BISQUE
(Bisque Aux Champignons)
¼ cup butter
½ pound fresh mushrooms, sliced
2 medium onions, finely chopped
1 garlic clove, minced
1 tablespoon fresh lemon juice
3 tablespoons flour
4 cups vegetarian bouillon (5 cubes)
2 teaspoons salt
¼ teaspoon ground black pepper

2 cups heavy whipping cream
Chopped parsley

Put mushrooms in cellophane bag and pour over them heavily salted boiling water. Close bag and hold with the hand, shake. Drain well, remove stems and chop them, but slice the caps. Heat butter and sauté mushrooms, onions and garlic for 4 or 5 minutes, stirring constantly. Sprinkle with lemon juice. Blend in the flour, then gradually stir in bouillon, salt and pepper. Cook, continuing to stir constantly until the mixture is thickened slightly. Stir in the cream, heat thoroughly. Sprinkle with parsley and serve immediately. Looks lovely in a soup tureen with ladle, or can be served in individual soup dishes.

SPINACH SOUFFLÉ

1 bunch fresh spinach
1 small onion, grated
3 level tablespoons flour
¾ cup milk
½ teaspoon salt
    Pinch of cayenne pepper

⅛ teaspoon nutmeg
4 egg yolks
7 egg whites stiffly beaten
   Grated Parmesan cheese

Thoroughly clean and stem the spinach. Spinach requires many rinsings to get all the sand from the crinkly leaves. Use only the small amount of water which clings to the leaves for cooking it.

Drain it well, rinse and coarsely chop the spinach.

In a saucepan, melt 3 tablespoons of butter. Grate 1 small onion into the butter and sauté lightly until onion is soft, but do not let brown. Then remove the pan from the heat and stir in 3 level tablespoons of flour. Gradually pour in ¾ cup of milk and season with ½ teaspoon salt and a tiny pinch of cayenne.

Place a small amount of the mixture in a blender and holding the top down firmly with the hand, blend it. Add a little more each time until the entire amount has been thoroughly mixed in the blender, then pour it all into a large bowl. Beat in the 4 egg yolks.

Preheat oven to 375° and prepare a well-greased six-cup soufflé dish.

Then gently fold in the 7 egg whites which have been beaten until they are stiff but not dry. Pour into the ready soufflé dish, sprinkle the top with grated Parmesan cheese and place in oven. Bake for 17 to 20 minutes, or until the soufflé is well risen, puffed and browned on the top. Serve at once!

COUNTRY MASHED POTATOES WITH PEARS
(Kartoffelstock Mit Birnen)
(Traditional rural food in all of German-speaking Switzerland)

6 pears, quartered, cored (apples can be substituted)
½ cup water
½ cup sugar
6 cups mashed potatoes
1 teaspoon ground cinnamon
1 whole clove
   Grated rind of ½ lemon
2 cups soft bread crumbs
⅓ cup butter, melted

Combine the pears, water, sugar, cinnamon, clove and lemon rind in a saucepan. Bring to a boil and simmer until the pears are tender. Remove the whole clove.

In a buttered 3-quart serving dish, place a layer of mashed potatoes. Add a layer of pears and 2 spoonsful of the sauce. Repeat in layers, ending with a layer of mashed potatoes and the remainder of the sauce. Brown the bread-crumbs in melted butter. Spoon over the mashed potatoes. This dish is especially liked by children.

SWISS CHARD FROM THE VAL DI BLENIO
(La Scarpaza Di Blenio)

1 bunch of fresh Swiss chard
1½ to 2 cups dry bread crumbs
  Package of Swiss cheese sliced
  Salt
  Flour
  Butter

Wash and clean the chard and chop or cut into fine pieces. Butter a baking dish and sprinkle it with fine dry bread crumbs. Put alternate layers of chard, thinly sliced Swiss cheese and a sprinkling of flour and salt. Sprinkle top layer with more bread crumbs and dot with butter. Bake in preheated oven at 350° for 15 minutes, or until vegetable is tender. Serves 4.

CHERRY PUDDING
(Chriesibrägel)

1½ cups hot milk
1½ cups stale white bread, broken in very small pieces
¼ cup butter
¼ cup sugar
2 eggs, well beaten
½ teaspoon cinnamon
1 teaspoon grated lemon rind
1 pound dark sweet cherries or 1½ cups canned dark sweet cherries well drained

Add hot milk to the bread crumbs, beat until smooth. Cream the butter and sugar together. Beat eggs into butter mixture. Stir in the cinnamon, lemon rind and mix in with milk and bread mixture; add cherries. Pour into a well-buttered 1½-quart baking dish. Bake in slow oven preheated to 325° for 30 minutes. Serve this dish warm.

TAHITI

Tahitian Buffet
Meatless Chicken à la King
Pulao
Citrus Salad
Curry Dressed Green Salad
Golden Compote
Toasted Pound Cake "Fingers"

ENTREE À LA KING

6 tablespoons butter
6 tablespoons sifted flour
1 teaspoon salt
  Dash white pepper
4 cups (1 quart) milk
2 13-oz. packages meatless chicken style, diced*
1 small jar sweet pimento
2 cups sliced mushrooms, sautéed in butter

Melt the butter, but do not let it brown. Into the melted butter sift the flour and mix quickly and thoroughly. Add the cold milk, salt and pepper. White pepper is used because specks of black pepper do not look attractive in a sauce. Place saucepan over low flame and stir constantly until the sauce begins to boil. Let boil for about 2 minutes, stirring all the time. This will remove the raw flour taste from the sauce.

Sauté the fresh sliced mushrooms in a small amount of butter until just done. Drain and rinse the pimento and dice. Add these two ingredients to sauce and stir. Fold in last the cubed chicken style. It crumbles easily so do not stir or boil.

Serve over toast points and garnish with a ripe olive on each point.

*Frozen slices so first defrost then cube. This product is made of peanut meal and soya protein. It can also be purchased in cans.

PULAO

2 cups rice uncooked
4 onions, thinly sliced
4 tablespoons golden seedless raisins
4 tablespoons slivered, blanched almonds
1 or 2 bay leaves
1½ cups butter
1 teaspoon cinnamon
1 cup cooked green peas
  Few cardamon seeds and a few strands of saffron

In a large skillet put half of the butter (¾ cup) and sauté the thinly sliced onions until just golden brown. Add the rice and the rest of the butter and sauté until the rice has absorbed most of the butter, stirring all the time. Add other ingredients and move to a large pot and cover with salted boiling water. Simmer slowly, covered, as rice swells and cooks. When all liquid is absorbed and rice is tender, sprinkle with the saffron and set in oven for 10 minutes before serving. Serves 6.

CITRUS SALAD

3 oranges, large size
2 large grapefruits
1 or 2 large avocados
  Lettuce leaves
  Oil and vinegar dressing

Peel oranges and slice into segments, removing membrane. Peel the 2 grapefruits and do the same. Hold fruit over bowl while cutting to catch the juice. Peel, halve and slice the avocados and dip the slices into the citrus juice to help prevent browning. Arrange the orange, grapefruit and avocado slices on lettuce leaves or on watercress. Chill. If you can get seedless white grapes this adds to the delight of the salad. Just before serving, drizzle with oil and vinegar dressing. Serves 6.

CURRY-DRESSING GREEN SALAD

Your own choice of iceberg, Bibb, Romaine, Ruby, Endive, or other lettuce and greens
¼ cup salad oil
2 tablespoons lemon or lime juice
½ teaspoon sugar
½ teaspoon Madras curry powder
  Dash of salt

Wash and drain the greens, and break into bite-sized pieces, toss together. Mix all other ingredients in jar with tight lid and shake to combine. Pour over greens and toss again and serve.

GOLDEN COMPOTE

2 cups preserved whole kumquats
1 can pineapple chunks
2 cans (about 11 oz. each) lichee nuts
1 tablespoon grated orange peel
1 tablespoon grated lemon peel
3 tablespoons lemon juice
1 cup fresh orange juice

Combine kumquats, pineapple and its juice, lichees and their juice and all other ingredients in saucepan. Bring to boil and simmer gently for about 20 minutes, uncovered, to reduce the liquid and blend the flavors. Cool and then chill in refrigerator. Serve chilled in stemmed compotes and accompany with Toasted Pound Cake Fingers.

TOASTED POUND CAKE FINGERS

Purchase a 1-lb. pound cake, pre-packaged or frozen will do. Cut 5 slices, each ¾-inch thick; then cut each slice in 4 lengthwise strips. Toast the cake strips, turning to lightly brown on all sides. This can be done while you are clearing the table before serving dessert. Serve hot or cooled. Serves 6.

TURKEY

Turkish Patio Buffet
Turkish Appetizers (Mezes)
Stuffed Green Peppers (Biber Dolmasi)
Stuffed Tomatoes (Domates Dolmasi)
Stuffed Oriental-type Eggplant (Patlijan Dolmasi)
Stuffed Grape Leaves (Yakprak Dolmasi)
Stuffed Cabbage Leaves (Lahana Dolmasi)
Choplet Nut Loaf
Mock Tel Kadayif
Turkish Delight (Turkish Paste)
Turkish Coffee

TURKISH APPETIZERS
(Called "Mezes")

A rice basic mixture is used to stuff vegetables called "dolmas" which dominate the menu—and the vegetables you use are fresh and succulent in September in America. These can be prepared the day before serving. In Turkey the cool dolmas are served as a first course. As this is a vegetarian menu I have improvised recipes, but flavor combinations are authentically Turkish.

STUFFED GREEN PEPPERS
"Biber Dolmasi"
(Bee-Bear Dolh-Mah-Suh)

12 to 15 small green peppers or halved
    medium-sized peppers
    Dolma Filling
1½ teaspoon salt

2 tablespoons olive oil
½ cup boiling water

Cut tops off the small green peppers, remove stems, but keep tops with matching peppers; remove seeds. Or cut the medium-sized peppers in half lengthwise through the stem. (Do not cut out stem end, it helps hold pepper in shape); fill each pepper about ⅞ full (Rice filling will expand,) Doma filling recipe will be at end of this menu. Put tops back on peppers or cover top of each pepper half with small piece of foil. Arrange peppers close together in heavy cast iron skillet and sprinkle salt and olive oil on tops, cover and simmer 25 to 30 minutes. (Add a little more water if needed; it should be almost cooked away when the vegetables are tender.) Cool in the pan, but can be served hot. One reason for preparing day ahead is one would not have enough pans for all the vegetables.

STUFFED TOMATOES
"Domates Dolmasi"
(Doh-Mah-Tes Dohl-Mah-Suh)

15   medium-small tomatoes
      (ripe, but very firm)
      Dolma Filling
1½ teaspoons salt
2   tablespoons olive oil
½   cup boiling water

Cut off tops of tomatoes, keeping tops with matching tomatoes; remove tomato pulp with a small spoon (this pulp can be used in the stuffing recipe). Stuff tomatoes about ⅞ full without packing. Put tops back on. It is best to use a rack in the bottom of the cooking pan for these—tomatoes hold their shape better if not resting in the water. Arrange the tomatoes close together on the rack in the cooking pan. Sprinkle salt and olive oil over the top. Pour boiling water down inside of pan. Cover and simmer until tomatoes are tender, 15 to 20 minutes, adding a little more water if needed. Cool in pan.

STUFFED ORIENTAL-TYPE EGGPLANT
"Patlijan Dolmasi"
(Paht-Luh-Jahn Dohl-Mah-Sah)

12   small finger-shaped eggplant
      or 2 regular eggplant
      Dolma filling
3   tablespoons olive oil
1½ teaspoons salt
½   cup water

Remove stems from small eggplants, cut in half, and use an apple corer to hollow out centers. The eggplant will look like a hollow tube, that is if you use the small ones; If you use the regular large eggplant, cut each in 6 wedges and carefully scoop out the pulp. Leave only enough pulp to hold shell firmly for filling — about ½-inch thick. For the Oriental-type eggplant make pockets for the filling. Stuff each eggplant about ⅞ full. (Rice filling will expand in the cooking.) Then cover the cut end of each with a small piece of foil. Arrange small eggplants close together in heavy cast iron skillet, cover and on very low heat simmer 25 to 30 minutes. Add a little water if needed; it should be almost cooked away when eggplants are tender. Cool to room temperature in pan.

STUFFED GRAPE LEAVES
"Yakprak Dolmasi"

Use fresh tender leaves of Thompson seedless grapes, or buy grape leaves preserved in brine from specialty store. 2½ dozen for 12 guests. Spoon filling onto grape leaf, arranged with stem end toward you. Veined side up. Fold over sides, roll from stem end toward you, veined side up. Fold over sides, roll from stem end. Arrange rolled grape leaves in the pan coated with olive oil. Set a heatproof plate on leaves. Add 1½ teaspoon salt with 2 tablespoons olive oil in ½ cup boilng water to heavy pan. Cover and simmer 25 to 30 minutes. Cool in pan and serve at room temperature.

STUFFED CABBAGE LEAVES
"Lahana Dolmasi"

15 Cabbage leaves, young

DOLMA FILLING

(Omit mint leaves and dill weed for cabbage.)
Follow directions given for grape leaves. Cook
separately in well oiled leaves; arrange filled,
roll seam down, side by side in heavy skillet.

DOLMA FILLING
"Dolma Ici" (Dohl-Mah EE-Chee)

6   cups boiling water
2   cups short grain rice (such as
    California Pearl)
1   cup olive oil
8   large onions, chopped
¼ to ½ cup Pine nuts
    (Pignolia purchased in nut stores)
4   teaspoons salt
2   large tomatoes, chopped, or 2 cups
    tomato pulp
2   cups boiling water
¼ to ½ cup currants or chopped raisins
1½ teaspoons each pepper and allspice
2   teaspoons sugar
1   tablespoon crushed dried mint leaves
1   tablespoon dillweed
    (Omit the last 2 ingredients for cabbage
    dolmas)

Pour the 6 cups boiling water over rice;
cover, and let stand until the water cools to
room temperature. Turn rice into a wire
strainer and run cold water through it, for a few
minutes; let the rice drain thoroughly.

In a large frying pan, heat olive oil. Add the
onions, pignolia nuts and salt; stir over
medium heat until the onions are golden
brown. Add the drained rice and continue to
stir until it browns lightly, about 10 minutes
more. Reduce heat to low and add tomatoes,
the 2 cups boiling water, currants, pepper,
allspice, sugar (keep out 15 tablespoons of
Dolma Filling for cabbage leaves before adding, mint and dill, if used). Heat and stir about 5
more minutes, until the rice has absorbed the
liquid. Remove from heat and turn on a platter
so rice will cool quickly. Makes about 10 cups
Dolma Filling, an ample amount to stuff 12 to
15 each small tomatoes, small peppers, Oriental finger-shaped eggplant, cabbage leaves,
and about 2½ dozen grape leaves—enough for
8 to 12 guests. Only one of the vegetables calls
for a variation (slight) of filling, omit the dill and
mint for the cabbage leaves, as mentioned before.

Plenty of lemon wedges should be on hand
for your guests to squeeze on the cabbage and
grape dolmas.

Each guest takes a selection or all five dolmas so that everyone can sample the different
types.

The filling for the Dolmas as well as the stuffed vegetables themselves may be made a day
ahead and kept in the refrigerator covered. At
least 1 or more hours before serving they
should be taken out of refrigerator as they are
served at room temperature.

The Choplet Nut Loaf can be served warm.

A large salad bowl with mixed fresh greens,
tossed with simple dressing of olive oil, vinegar, salt and pepper should be on the buffet
for each guest to help himself.

Greek bakeries and delicatessens in the
large cities of America carry Armenian cracker

bread, called "Lavash". If it is not available in your area, serve crusty French bread.

CHOPLET NUT LOAF

1 (20-ounce) can vegetarian choplets purchased in health food stores
1 cup nut meats
½ cup dried bread crumbs
1 onion, chopped
2 eggs, beaten
1 teaspoon salt
¼ cup melted butter or oil
1 tablespoon vegetarian bouillon paste dissolved in 1 cup hot water
3 bay leaves

Put choplets, nuts, bread, and onion through chopper (grinder). Mix eggs, salt, oil; add to ground mixture. Add broth; mix well. Place bay leaves on top of loaf. Bake in a 350°F. oven for 1½ hours. Remove bay leaves and allow to stand for 10 minutes before serving and cutting.

PATIO TURKISH BUFFET

Frequently harvest small green peppers from your garden, but you can use halved regular sized peppers. For grape leaves, use fresh tender leaves of Thompson seedless grapes, or buy grape leaves preserved in brine from a specialty food store.

Even though the same filling is used, each stuffed vegetable is cooked separately. The filling takes on a distinct taste in each vegetable, so do not mix the flavors by cooking several kinds together. The vegetables have different cooking times and should not be overcooked or they will lose their shape.

Olive oil is essential to the flavor of these vegetables, so do not substitute another salad oil, or butter or margarine, which will solidify when cold. The prepared vegetables can be kept in the refrigerator, but must be taken out about one hour before serving. They are intended to be served at room temperature.

One basic rice mixture is used to stuff the following vegetables, but surprisingly different flavors result when they cook. The small eggplants are found in markets that sell Italian or Oriental foods. You can use regular eggplant if you prefer home gardens.

MOCK TEL KADAYIF

6 large shredded wheat biscuits
   About 1½ cups boiling water
¾ cup chopped walnuts
½ cup butter (1 stick), melted
1 cup water
1 cup sugar
1 teaspoon lemon juice
   Light or heavy cream (optional)

Place each biscuit on a slotted spoon and dip in the boiling water; remove quickly and drain on a wire rack. Wrap biscuits in foil and chill about 4 hours. Cut each biscuit in half lengthwise and arrange on lower section in a buttered 8-inch baking dish. Sprinkle lower section with walnuts; cover with the top sections. Pour melted butter over the biscuits. Bake at 350°F. for 20 minutes, or until lightly browned.

In a saucepan combine sugar and water. Bring to a boil and let it boil rapidly for 5 min-

157

utes; add lemon juice. Take the dessert out of the oven and pour the prepared syrup over the biscuits. If you wish, pour cream on top.

This is the mock "Tel Kadayif" exotic dessert recipe—traditional dish of the near east or rather an adaptation of a recipe from that part of the world.

Tel Kadayif is a Turkish dessert made with a thread-like pasta, walnuts and a sweet syrup. You may be surprised to find that the familiar American breakfast food, shredded wheat, is used in this adaptation.

DESSERT
"Turkish Delight"

Also known as "Turkish Paste". It is a sweetmeat of Turkish origin, usually consisting of gelatinous, fruit-flavored cubes coated with powdered sugar. This is the way to make it:

2 tablespoons agar agar (seaweed gelatin) or other vegetarian gelatin can be used
½ cup cold water
¾ cup fruit juice or part juice and part boiling water to make ¾ cup
2 cups sugar
1 tablespoon lemon juice
1 teaspoon vanilla extract
Food coloring

Soak 2 tablespoons agar agar (or other vegetarian gelatin) in ½ cup cold water. Add ¾ cup fruit juice or boiling water and pour mixture into saucepan. Add 2 cups sugar and on slow heat, bring it to the boiling point and the sugar has dissolved.

Boil quickly for about 10 minutes to make a syrup. Remove from the heat and add 1 tablespoon lemon juice and 1 teaspoon vanilla — or other flavoring if you prefer.

If you used orange or raspberry juice in the recipe, you will not need to add food coloring, but if you did not you might want to add a few drops of color at this point.

Pour into a shallow square pan to harden. Cut with knife that has been dipped in boiling water to heat the blade. Then roll each cube in powdered or granulated sugar.

Be sure to use full strength fruit juices in this recipe, not diluted ones.

TURKISH COFFEE

Also known as Armenian or Greek coffee. Traditionally made in a copper "Ibrik", a tapering pot with a handle and open at the top, but can be made in a saucepan or uncovered percolator pot instead. (There are various sizes of "Ibriks" from 2 to 10 cups.)

If you are enthusiastic about Turkish coffee, you may want to invest in a Turkish coffee mill. They are handsome cylinders, in which you can grind coffee beans by hand. You often see Turkish ibriks in import shops. Cinnamon flavored, sweetened Turkish coffee, already powdered, is available in jars. Sweetened Turkish coffee has become a favorite of many westerners.

Genuine Turkish coffee is made with pulverized coffee. At a coffee roasting house, ask to have some of your favorite kinds of beans very finely ground for Turkish coffee.

Method:

Measure 1½ cups cold water into an "Ibrik", a saucepan or similar container. Add 4 teaspoons sugar and heat. When water has boiled, stir in pulverized coffee. Bring to a boil, allow to froth up, and remove from heat for a moment. The frothing process is repeated 2 more times. Many Americans prefer their coffee a little milder so froth up only once and taste it first. Without stirring, add a few drops of cold water to settle the grounds. Have Demitasse cups ready and spoon some of the foam into each cup, then pour in the coffee. Makes 4 Demitasse servings

UNITED STATES OF AMERICA

Wild Rice Casserole
Fried Apples
Acorn Squash
Yankee Corn Bread
or
Southern Corn Bread
Tossed Salad with Buttermilk Dressing
Pecan Pie

MINNESOTA
WILD RICE CASSEROLE

2 cups wild rice
4 cups boiling water
4 envelopes of instant bouillon or broth mix
½ cup butter
Slivered almonds
1 cup onion, chopped
1 cup celery, chopped
2 cloves garlic, pressed
2 3-oz. cans mushrooms, sliced and broiled in butter

Wash rice well and place in a four-quart casserole. Dissolve the bouillon cubes or packets in boiling water and pour over the rice. Let stand 2 to 3 hours. Heat oven to 350°. Melt butter in a skillet over moderately low heat; add onion and celery and sauté gently; add garlic and continue to stir occasionally until cooked and tender. Pick out the pressed garlic cloves and discard. Add mushrooms and sautéed vegetables to the rice and mix together carefully. Cover the casserole and bake for 30 minutes. Remove from oven and let stand 5 minutes before serving. Garnish the top with almonds and serve.

WASHINGTON
FRIED APPLES

6 greening apples, or other firm, cooking apples
1 stick butter
2 cups brown sugar
Cinnamon and nutmeg to taste

Peel, core and slice the apples. Melt butter in a heavy skillet and add the brown sugar, stirring constantly to make a caramel sauce. Add apples, continue to stir until apples are tender and completely permeated with the sugar syrup. Serve in covered dish.

VERMONT
ACORN SQUASH

½ squash for each guest
Butter
Honey

Select well-formed squash, not too large. Halve them and clean out seeds. Lightly sprinkle each half with a pinch of salt. Then in the center of each half, put 1 to 1½ tablespoons of honey and a pat of butter. Place in baking dish with just enough water to cover the bottom of the pan and bake in oven at 350° for 45 minutes. Serve as baked in the shells.

YANKEE CORN BREAD

1 cup flour
1 teaspoon salt
2½ teaspoons baking powder
2 to 4 tablespoons sugar
¾ cup yellow corn meal
1 egg
1 cup milk
4 tablespoons melted butter or shortening

Sift flour, salt, baking powder, sugar and cornmeal together. Add the unbeaten egg and milk; stir quickly and lightly until mixed. Stir in the melted butter. Pour batter into one or two well-greased, shallow pans; it should not be more than ¾ inch deep. Bake in hot oven (400°) for 20 minutes to 30 minutes. Leftover cornbread is very good toasted.

SOUTHERN CORN BREAD, CORN MUFFINS OR CORN STICKS

2 cups water-ground cornmeal
1 teaspoon salt
½ teaspoon soda
1½ teaspoons baking powder
1 tablespoon sugar, optional
2 eggs
1½ cups buttermilk
¼ cup melted butter or shortening

If you are making corn bread, use a 9″ x 9″ cake pan; if you are making muffins, this recipe will make 18 3-in. muffins or 18 corn sticks.

Pans for baking corn bread, muffins, or corn sticks should be greased generously and put in the oven while it is being preheated to baking temperature of 400°. If you prefer thin corn bread, you may use a larger pan or use two 8″ x 8″ pans. Sift the cornmeal, salt, soda, baking powder and sugar into a mixing bowl. Stir in the unbeaten eggs, buttermilk and melted butter or shortening; stir only until batter is well-mixed. It should be lumpy. Pour the batter into the pan. For muffins or corn sticks, they should be filled ⅔ full.

Bake at 400° about 30 minutes. If not brown on top, place under the broiler for a few minutes.

WISCONSIN BUTTERMILK SALAD DRESSING

1 cup cultured buttermilk
1 cup mayonnaise (do not substitute)
1 rounded teaspoon salt
¼ teaspoon pepper
½ teaspoon dill weed
½ teaspoon lemon flavored salad seasonings
½ teaspoon dried parsley, crushed fine

Start with the mayonnaise then add buttermilk to it gradually to make it smooth. Add the seasonings and for your own variations, you can add from ⅛ to ¼ teaspoon of other favorite seasonings crushed fine, such as basil, oregano, thyme, curry powder, mint or crumbled blue cheese. Put in jar and chill until time to serve. Shake bottle or stir with spoon; do not use mixer or blender with this dressing.

CALIFORNIA TOSSED SALAD

1 bunch well-washed and veined fresh raw spinach, broken into bite size
1 sweet onion, sliced thin and separated into rings
2 or 3 tomatoes, quartered or use whole cherry tomatoes
12 to 15 cauliflower flowerettes
1 cup drained canned garbanzo beans
Cucumbers, radishes and celery to taste

Toss and add buttermilk dressing, serve in salad bowls.

GEORGIA PECAN PIE

½ cup sugar or ½ cup brown sugar firmly packed
¾ cup white corn syrup (must use corn syrup)
2 tablespoons honey
½ stick of butter softened or melted
3 eggs, slightly beaten
1 teaspoon vanilla
1 to 2 cups pecans, halves or broken meats

For Pastry recipe see Index or buy pre-made frozen ones already in a baking tin. Put aside until filling is prepared.

Preheat oven to 350°.

In small mixing bowl, mix sugar, corn syrup and honey. Stir in softened or melted butter. Add slightly beaten eggs and vanilla. If you are using broken nut meats, add them to the mixture at this point. If you intend to use perfect ones, pour the mixture into the pie shell and arrange the halves on top, completely covering it. Or again, you may want to mix broken nuts into the filling and a layer of the perfect halves to decorate the top. Bake for 45 minutes in 350° oven and let cool before cutting to serve.

This recipe is particularly interesting as variations will not hurt the ultimate product. You may use one or both kinds of the sugar; you may leave out the honey, or substitute more sugar in place of the syrup. Just do not use other types of syrup such as maple, the results will not be the same. If you prefer a richer pie, you may use more butter. You can make it with 4 small eggs or two very large ones rather than the 3 called for above. But keeping the ingredients more or less in balance, you will always have a good and a very simple pie.

KANSAS CORN PUDDING

2 cups (No. 303 can) creamstyle corn
3 eggs or 6 egg yolks
2 cups milk
1 teaspoon salt
Few grains cayenne pepper
1 tablespoon melted butter

Beat the egg, add milk, seasonings, melted butter and corn. Turn the mixture into a shallow, buttered baking dish (1½ qt. size). Place baking dish in a pan of hot water in 350° oven for about 1 hour, or until the pudding will not adhere to a knife inserted 1″ from edge of dish. Serves 4.

VIRGIN ISLANDS

Menu for Luncheon
Fresh Fruit Compote
Sour Cream Pimento Soufflé
Sautéed Vegetarian Sausages
Okra Creole   Dilled Carrots
Herbed Tomatoes
St. Croix Island Sundae

FRESH FRUIT COMPOTE

Using oranges, sweet limes, any kind of melons in season with bananas, berries, plums, apricots, or whatever is available fresh. Peel and cut fruit into bite size. When using bananas wait to add them just before serving as they turn dark. Sugar to taste—approximately ¼ cup—and add 1 teaspoon artificial rum flavoring. Mix well and chill for 4 hours before serving in sherbet glasses with a sprig of mint in each.

SOUR CREAM PIMENTO SOUFFLÉ

4   tablespoons butter
4   tablespoons flour
¾   teaspoon salt
¾   cup light cream
¾   cup sour cream
⅛   teaspoon paprika
⅛   teaspoon dry mustard
2   cans (or jars) sliced pimentos (4 oz. each)
8   egg yolks and 6 egg whites
¼   teaspoon cream of tartar

Melt butter in frying pan and stir in the flour, salt, paprika and mustard. Gradually and smoothly, stir in the light cream, then the sour cream, stirring until thickened. Blend in the pimentos. Beat a little of this hot mixture into the lightly beaten egg yolks, then pour eggs back into the pan and remove from the heat. Beat the egg whites with cream of tartar until they hold a peak. Fold the beaten egg whites into the other mixture. Pour mixture into a well buttered 2-quart casserole (may be wide and shallow or deep with straight sides). At this point you can chill the soufflé as long as two hours, but it is preferable to bake immediately in an oven preheated to 375° for 25 to 30 minutes, or until the soufflé is nicely browned and feels firm when tapped lightly in the center. (Inside of the soufflé should be moist.) Serve immediately!

SAUTÉED VEGETARIAN SAUSAGES

These products can be purchased in supermarkets and are widely available. They need only to be heated or sautéed quickly in butter or oil.

OKRA CREOLE

1 lb. okra
1 green pepper, sliced
2 onions
1 teaspoon salt
1 cup canned tomatoes
1 clove garlic
2 tablespoons butter

Clean okra, cut off ends. Place in saucepan and pour boiling water over it. Bring it to a boil again, then drain off this water; this eliminates any of the slimy consistency often encountered with cooked okra. Slice onions top to bottom (instead of around) into narrow strips; slice green peppers into pieces about the same size as the onion—approximately 1½ to 2 inches long by ¼ inch width. Peel garlic clove and place in skillet with the butter. Fry green peppers and onions in garlic butter for a few minutes, taking care not to let butter scorch. Add tomatoes and okra into skillet and simmer until okra is done. This can be served immediately with or without a topping of toasted bread crumbs.

DILLED CARROTS

8 to 10 new carrots
½ cup white vinegar
½ cup water
1 teaspoon dill weed
1 teaspoon celery salt

Peel and cut carrots into sticks and simmer, covered, for 15 minutes. If you prefer, you may steam them so that they are lightly cooked, but still freshly crisp. Mix water, vinegar, dill weed and celery salt together. Pour over the drained carrot sticks and marinate overnight in refrigerator.

HERBED TOMATOES

4 tomatoes, medium size, peeled and sliced
2 tablespoons minced green onions
2 tablespoons minced fresh parsley
1 tablespoon basil, crushed
   Brown sugar
   French Dressing

Peel and slice tomatoes into large soup plate. Sprinkle brown sugar lightly over tomatoes and follow with the mixed herbs, making sure all the dish is herbed. Drizzle bottled French dressing over the whole dish and marinate for several hours as it chills in refrigerator before serving.

ST. CROIX ISLAND SUNDAE

1½ quarts coffee ice cream
8   oz. flaked coconut
2   cups chocolate topping

Spread the coconut in a shallow baking pan and toast in 350° oven for about 10 minutes. Scoop 12 ice cream balls and roll each immediately in coconut and place in freezer compartment of the refrigerator.

PRACTICAL TIPS FROM A FRENCH COOK

Tip #1: To keep egg yolks fresh and moist, place the unbroken yolks in cold water. Have sufficient water in the cup or bowl to cover the yolks. They will keep perfectly without drying out.

Tip #2: To make sweet cream sour, just add 2 teaspoons of lemon juice for each cup of sweet cream. To each cup of evaporated milk, add 1 teaspoon of vinegar. This tip is useful when you do not have the sour cream required for a recipe.

Tip #3: To cook dried beans and eliminate distress after eating, use about a teaspoon of baking soda in the water they are boiled in and the gas that causes distress will be eliminated. Baking soda also eliminates gas from cabbage.

Tip #4: To cook Broccoli, Brussels Sprouts, Cabbage and Cauliflower without an odor, start them in boiling water and leave the kettle uncovered. This will also improve the appearance, flavor and digestibility of those vegetables as well. Put 1 teaspoon of baking soda in the boiling water and cook for only 3 minutes. Pour off the soda water and replace with fresh water to which 1 teaspoon of salt per quart is added. Boil vegetable until tender, for cabbage it is only 7 to 10 minutes, but test vegetable with fork. Another method to eliminate the odor when cooking these vegetables is to cook a stalk of celery with them.

Tip #5: To remove yolk from egg white or when separating yolks from whites, use part of an egg shell. You will find that yolk can easily be taken out. It is important to remove any least trace of yolk if the white is to be beaten; it cannot be removed any other way.

Tip #6: How to remove excessive salt from soups? Drop into it sliced raw potato and boil for 5 to 6 minutes. The potato will extract some of the salt. The amount of potato used will depend on how salty the soup is. Or you may use a pinch of brown sugar in soup made too salty; the salt will be overcome by the brown sugar, but will have no sweet taste.

Tip #7: To keep rice, macaroni, or other pasta from boiling over, grease the top 3 or 4 inches inside of the pan and the water will not boil over onto the stove.

Tip #8: A rule to remember which tells you how to cook any vegetable is to remember how it grows. If it grows beneath the ground, covered in the cold earth (a root vegetable) then start it in cold water and cover the pot with a lid. That is for potatoes, turnips, carrots, or any underground vegetable.

If it grows above the ground, uncovered in the sun, then start it in boiling water and leave the pot uncovered. The rule is to cook them as they grow, until they are crisp and tender, not until they are mushy and overdone.

Tip #9: To keep lemons fresh in the refrigerator rather than having the skins dry out, fill a quart jar with cold water and drop the lemons in so that the water completely covers them. Use a jar that seals tightly with a rubber ring under the cap. Put the lid on tightly and the lemons will keep indefinitely.

Tip #10: To keep brown sugar from becoming hard, store it in a canning jar with rubber seal. The moisture will be kept in the sugar and it will not harden. If brown sugar has hardened, place it in the oven at low heat, 250° to 325°, until it softens enough to use.

Tip #11: To prevent a drinking glass or glass dish from breaking when it is being filled with hot liquid, just put a metal spoon into it before pouring the liquid in. The metal spoon helps absorb the heat. If you will also make sure the glass dish is not especially cold, this will also avoid the chance of breaking.

Tip #12: To prevent candles from smoking when extinguished, bend the tip of the wick over so that it goes into the hot wax. This can be done with a burnt matchstick. Then when you blow out the candle there will be no smoke. It is the lack of wax at the tip of the wick that causes the smoke.

Tip #13: To remove the skin easily from peaches and tomatoes, place fruit in a large spoon and lower it into boiling water for a few seconds. The skin will then peel off easily without the fresh taste of the peach being affected. The tomato can be done the same way after first removing the stem mark from it. Or another way you can use with tomatoes is to insert a fork in the stem end and slowly turn the tomato over an open flame. The skin will peel off easily and the tomato will still be cold!

Tip #14: Lemons will yield more juice if they are placed in hot water two or three minutes before squeezing.

Tip #15: To prevent eggs from breaking when being boiled puncture the round (large) end of the egg by sticking a pin or thumb tack barely through the shell. This allows the escape of air from the egg. It is the expanding air that causes the shell to break. It is important to lower the egg into the boiling water with a large spoon; do not drop it into the water. If you are hardboiling eggs, it minimizes breakage to dip them each first into cold water before putting them into the boiling water.

Tip #16: To make scrambled eggs creamy, cook them in the top of a double boiler rather than a skillet. Stir gently every few seconds.

Tip #17: In recipes that call for sour milk (or buttermilk) and baking soda, you may safely substitute if you find you only have sweet, fresh milk on hand. With sweet milk, use 2 level teaspoons of baking powder for each cup of flour the recipe calls for. The results are the same as if you had used soda and sour milk.

Tip #18: To make cake flour from all-purpose flour simply sift the recipe amount called for five times. Cake flour is a finer texture than regular flour, but this ploy will work if you use a good brand of ordinary flour.

Tip #19: To keep nuts and fruits from sinking to the bottom of cakes, etc., heat them in the oven, then roll them in a little flour before adding them to the batter.

Tip #20: To boil an egg that is cracked, wrap it in waxed paper, twisting the ends to keep it on the egg and boil with the paper on.

Tip #21: Dried prunes are sold by size. Many cooks do not know that small prunes which cost less than the large ones contain practically as much pulp. The small prunes have small seeds while the larger ones have very large seeds. This can be quite a saving while buying equal quality.

Tip #22: To cook corn on the cob, boil only 3 minutes. You cannot make corn soft and tender by boiling it 20 minutes or longer any more than you can make an egg softer by boiling it longer. Place corn ears into fast boiling water with no lid and *no salt*. You'll be delighted with it's fresh tender taste at no more than 3 minutes boiling time. Try it.

Tip #23: Remember to keep spices and herbs stored away from your stove or other source of heat. They deteriorate fastest near the stove where both heat and moisture are generated. It is even better to store them away from light.

Tip #24: Cut green beans, celery, and other vegetables diagonally for more flavor! The Chinese have long known this secret and that it unlocks more of the flavor of a vegetable than does a straight cut. Also it is easier to cut green beans either diagonally or lengthwise (French cut) by using kitchen scissors and much quicker, too.

Tip #25: When peeling onions, save your tears by putting a piece of bread between your teeth. The odor of onion can be removed from hands by rinsing them in cold water; if it persists, lemon juice will remove the last bit of onion odor from the hands.

Notes on Vegetarian Ingredients

In vegetarian cooking many recipes call for protein meat substitutes, vegetarian stocks and seasonings, gravy and soup bases and gelatin substitutes. We have tried in INTERNATIONAL VEGETARIAN CUISINE to avoid the use of brand names. Often a brand which is familiar in one section of the country is unknown and unavailable in another.

To help you to substitute for any such ingredients in this book, we give you a partial list with descriptions of some of these.

VEGETARIAN STOCKS, SEASONINGS AND GRAVY BASES

Savita - extract (vegetable)
Vegex - cubes or extract (vegetable)
Tastex - extract (vegetable)

VEGETABLE PROTEIN MEAT SUBSTITUTES

Wham - canned, smoked flavor like ham
Choplets - beef style
Soyameat - Chicken style or beef style
Protose - texture like bread
Numete - light, to be sliced in rounds
Vegemix - dry mix for patties or meat loaf
Ham
Bacon - Morning Star Brands, frozen
Sausage

VEGETARIAN GELATIN SUBSTITUTES (no animal tissue)

Jell-Quick - found in Kosher foods section
Agar-agar

GELATIN: The gelatin we advise in this book is pure vegetable gelatin made of seaweed which is found in the depths of the ocean near Sri Lanka (Ceylon).

One importance lies in the inherent vitaman value. There is no difference in taste from the ordinary animal-derived gelatin, but the seaweed gelatin, or agar-agar, sets much more quickly. Seaweed gelatin is available in most health food stores.

YOGURT: Most commercial yogurts purchased in markets in this country is not pure yogurt. Most name brands contain animal-gelatin, food coloring, added starch, and chemical preservatives. It is much better to make your own yogurt at home. The starter, acidophilus, is a bacteria which is very good for you, even to the extent that its presence in buttermilk, sweet milk, yogurt, or clabber will destroy harmful bacteria in the stomach and intestines.

SPROUTS: The craze for alfalfa sprouts has been greatly over-rated and it has been proven that these are not as beneficial as other greens. This information comes from research done by recognized nutritionists. Though there is nurishment in sprouts, one should not go overboard about eating them to the exclusion of other good foods. Pseudo healthfood cults do not help the cause of the true vegetarian with freak diets and lack of normal balance in eating.

Index

Cantaloupe with Honey ....Greece
Cantaloupe, Ice Cream ....Australia
Cantonese Sauce ....China
Caper Sauce ....Netherlands, Hawaii
Caponata.......................................Italy
Caramel Custard ....Mexico
Carrot Salad ....China
Carrots ....Australia
Carrots, Dilled ....Virgin Is.
Cauliflower Soup...........................Egypt
Celery, Braised .....................G.B.-England
Celery Hearts, Olives ....Portugal
Celery Root Marinade ....Morocco
Chantilly Dressing ....Philippine Is.
Chard, Swiss ....Switzerland
Cheese Cake.......................New Zealand
Cheese Croquettes ....Netherlands
Cheese Fritters ....Finland
Cheese Pudding ....Germany
Cheese Rarebit .....................G.B.-Wales
Cheese Sauce..................Brazil, Denmark
Cheese Souffle ....France
Cherry Pudding ....Germany, Switzerland
Cherry Velvet Cream ....Indonesia
Chicken Salad, Meatless ....Indonesia
Chicken a la King, Meatless ....Tahiti
Chicken Malaysian, Meatless ....Philippine Is.
Chicken. Meatless, Rings ....Argentina
Chicory Boats...........................Spain
Chicory Salad ....Netherlands
Chilaquiles (Scrambled Eggs) ....Mexico
Chiles Rellenos ....Mexico
Chloduik ....Poland
Chocolate Mousse ....Netherlands
Choplet Nut Loaf.........................Turkey
Chutney ....India
Citrus Salad ....Tahiti
Coconut, Fried............................India
Coconut Milk ....Indonesia
Coffee Bavarian Cream ....Germany
Cold Summer Soup ....Poland
Condiment Tray for Curry ....India
Copenhagen Lima Beans ....Denmark

Corn Bread, Corn Bread, (Southern, Yankee) .U.S.
Corn Chowder ....Bahama Is.
Corn Pie (Pastel de Choclo) ....Argentina
Cottage Cheese, Fruit ....Canada
Cottage Cheese, Tomato Salad ....Hungary
Cream Cheese Ramekins ....Austria
Creamed Onions ....Russia
Creamed Spinach ....Australia, Ireland
Creamy Vanilla Frosting ....Austria
Crepes ....France
Crepe, Fillings ....France
Crescent Rolls ....New Zealand
Croissants ....France
Croutons ....France
Currant Buns ......................G.B.-England
Curry-Dressed Salad ....Tahiti
Curry Dressing ....Hawaii, Indonesia
Cucumber Salad ....Spain
Cucumber in Dill.........................Ireland
Cucumbers, Baked ....Brazil
Cucumbers Viennese....................Austria
Custard, Danish ....Denmark
Custard, Flan ....Spain
Custard, Spiced (Jericalla) ....Mexico
Dahl.......................................India
Danish Custard ....Denmark
Danish Fruit Soup ....Denmark
Date Crunch Torte ....Morocco
Devonshire Strawberries ..........G.B.-England
Dill Dip Tray ....Jamaica
Dilled Carrots ....Virgin Islands
Dolmasi (Stuffed Vegetables) ....Turkey
"Duck Sauce" ....China
Egg Casserole, Cheese Sauce ....Denmark
Egg Foo Yong ....China
Egg-Lemon Soup ....Greece
Eggplant Patties ....Arabia
Eggplant, Stuffed ....Egypt, Italy, Turkey
Eggplant Rigati ....Italy
Egg Rissoles, Ukrainian ....Russia
Eggs, Spanish Style ....Spain
Eggs, Stuffed ....Argentina
Eggs with Caper Sauce ......Hawaii, Netherlands

El Rancho Salad........................Mexico
Endive, Braised....................G.B.-England
Ensalada de Pocho...................Argentina
Ensalada Russa.....................Argentina
Falafel with Sauce......................Israel
Farina Pudding.........................Egypt
Fassouliahnia, White Beans.............Bulgaria
Filled Turnip Cups......................Poland
Finnish Easter Bread...................Finland
Finnish Summer Soup...................Finland
Flan, Custard..........................Spain
Fluffy Fruit Dressing..................Jamaica
French Vanilla Ice Cream...........Philippine Is.
French Onion Soup.....................France
Fresh Mushroom Bisque............Switzerland
Fried Apples..............................U.S.
Fried Avocado..........................Hawaii
Frijoles Refritos.......................Mexico
Fruit, Vegetable Gelatin..................Greece
Fruit Compote.......................Virgin Is.
Fruit Fool.........................G.B.-England
Fruit Plate Combinations, Six.......Philippine Is.
Fruit Rice Pudding....................Hungary
Fruit Sauce...........................Belgium
Fruit Soup...........................Denmark
Gado Gado...........................Indonesia
Garlic French Bread.................Netherlands
Gazpacho..............................Spain
German Cherry Pudding................Germany
German Potato-Carrot Soup............Germany
Ginger Ice Cream.....................Canada
Ginger Pears.........................Bulgaria
Glazed Parsnips.......................Finland
Golden Compote.......................Tahiti
Grape Leaves, Stuffed.................Turkey
Grapefruit Ginger Mold................Jamica
Gravy for Nut Roast..................Australia
Greek Pastries........................Greece
Green Beans in Custard..................Japan
Green Bean Salad..................Netherlands
Green Beans, Diced Carrots........New Zealand
Green Goddess Dressing................Hawaii
Green Pea Salad......................Morocco
Green Pea Soup....................Netherlands

Green Peas, New Potatoes...............Poland
Greens Pie..............................Greece
Green Peppers, Stuffed..........Canada, Turkey
Guacamole Dressing.....................Mexico
Guava Fruit Punch......................Mexico
Halva...................................India
Hard Eggs, Caper Sauce......Hawaii, Netherlands
Hardcooked Eggs, Red....................Greece
Herbed Tomatoes.....................Virgin Is.
Hollandaise Sauce......................France
Homemade Biscuit Tortoni.................Italy
Homemade Tomato Soup.............New Zealand
Iced Tea, Mint (see Lemon Balm).........Jamaica
Irish Soda Bread.......................Ireland
Island Pot Pie..........................Hawaii
Jellied Apples.........................Finland
Jericalla...............................Mexico
Jerusalem Salad.........................Israel
Jollof Rice.............................Ghana
Kedgeree..........................G.B.-Wales
King Kamehameha Pie....................Hawaii
Kiwi Fruit.........................New Zealand
Kofta Bread............................Arabia
Koftesi................................Arabia
Kulich, Quick..........................Russia
Kumquats...............................China
Kuri Rice..............................Japan
Lasagne.................................Italy
Latke..................................Israel
Leek Casserole....................G.B.-Wales
Legume et Noix Loaf.....................Iran
Lemon Balm Iced Tea....................Hawaii
Lemon Butter Squash...................Portugal
Lemon Curd........................G.B.-England
Lemon Glaze............................Russia
Lemon-Honey Dressing...................Canada
Lemon-Egg Soup.........................Greece
Lichee, Avocado Salad...................China
Lima Beans............................Denmark
Little Cold Summer Soup.................Poland
Macaroni Shells, Spinach.................Italy
Macaroni, Sweet Basil....................Italy
Macedoine Salad......................Bulgaria
Malaysian Chicken..................Philippine Is.

Marinated Celery Root ....Morocco	Oriental Sundae Sauce ....China
Marrow, Baked Vegetable .........G.B.-England	Palm Soup ....Ghana
Mashed Potatoes and Pears ....Switzerland	Pancakes, Swedish ....Sweden
Mayonnaise...............................France	Pancakes (see Crepes) ....France
Meatless Chicken a la King ....Tahiti	Papaya, Baked ....Hawaii
Meatless Chicken Malaysian ....Philippines	Parsleyed Potatoes ....Portugal
Meatless Chicken Rings ....Argentina	Parsnips in Drawn Butter ....Finland
Mediterranean Salad ....Egypt	Parsnips, Glazed ....Finland
Melon Compote............................Iran	Pastel de Choclo ....Argentina
Mezes (see Dolmasi, Appetizers) ....Turkey	Pastry Pockets (Pierogi) ....Poland
Middle East Salad ....Iran	Pastry Shell.............................France
Miso Soup................................Japan	Pastries, Greek ....Greece
Mock Chicken Salad ....Indonesia	Peanut Sauce ....Indonesia
Mock Tel Kadayif ....Turkey	Peanut Soup ....Ghana
Mornay Sauce ....Belgium	Peace Ginger Dessert....................Arabia
Moussaka ....Greece	Peach Macaroon Mold .............G.B.-Wales
Mousse, Chocolate ....Netherlands	Peach Melba ....Italy
Mushroom Bisque ....Switzerland	Peach Tapioca ....Australia
Mushroom-Oatmeal Patties .......G.B.-Scotland	Pears, Poached.......................Bulgaria
Mushroom Pudding ....Finland	Peas, New Potatoes ....Poland
Mushroom Salad ....Germany	Peas and Rice Aloha ....Hawaii
Mushroom Sauce ....Jamaica	Pecan Pie ..............................U.S.
Mushroom Tetrazinni ....Italy	Peppers, Stuffed ....Canada
Nasi Goreng (Rice Dish) ....Indonesia	Pickled Beets and Onions ....Russia
New Zealand Salad.................New Zealand	Pierogi ....Poland
Nkrakra Soup ....Ghana	Pineapple Salad ....Hawaii
Nut Brittle ....Sweden	Plantanos ....Mexico
Nut Brittle Pudding ....Sweden	Poached Ginger Pears ....Bulgaria
Nut Croquettes ....Sweden	Poppy Seed Cake ....Austria
Nut Roast..........................New Zealand	Portuguese Eggs ....Portugal
Nutmeat Loaf .....................G.B.-England	Pot de Creme au Chocolat ....Portugal
Oatmeal-Mushroom Patties .......G.B.-Scotland	Pot Pie, Island ....Hawaii
Okra Creole ....Virgin Islands	Potato-Carrot Soup ....Germany
Olive Stuffed Tomatoes ....Jamaica	Potato Loaf ....Ireland
Onion Soup ....France	Potato-Pear, Mashed ....Switzerland
Onions, Creamed........................Russia	Potato Pancakes ....Israel
Orange Glazed Bananas ....Jamaica	Potatoes, with New Peas ....Poland
Orange Pecan Muffins ....Bahama Is.	Pound Cake Fingers....................Tahiti
Orange Sandwich Bread ....Canada	Prune Whip ....Finland
Orange Sauce ....Bahama Is.	Pulao (Rice) ....India, Tahiti
Orange Sherbet ....Hawaii	Quiche Lorraine ....France
Oriental Eggs ....Japan	Raw Carrot with Sauce ....China
Oriental Patties ....Hungary	Red Hardcooked Eggs ....Greece

Refritos, Frijoles ....Mexico	Squash, Acorn...............................U.S.
Relish Plate ....Mexico	Squash, Lemon-Butter ....Portugal
Rice Brazilian ....Brazil	Steamed Beet Tops ....Bulgaria
Rice, Jollof..............................Ghana	Stewed Tomatoes ....Netherlands
Rice, Pulao ....India, Tahiti	Stock; Basic Broth ....France
Rice Savoury...........................Hawaii	Strawberries Devonshire ...........G.B.-England
Rice-Stuffed Cabbage ....Russia	Stuffed Cabbage Leaves ....Turkey
Rice-Stuffed Tomatoes ....Greece	Stuffed Grape Leaves ....Turkey
Rice, Walnut, Loaf ....Belgium	Stuffed Green Peppers..........Canada, Turkey
Ricotta Cheese Pancakes ....Italy	Stuffed Eggplant ....Egypt, Turkey
Rigati-Eggplant Bake ....Italy	Stuffed Tomato ....Greece, Turkey
Rissoles, Ukrainian Egg ....Russia	Stuffed Tomato Salad ....Philippine Is.
Rissotto Al Funghi ....Italy	Sukiyaki ....Japan
Russian Dressing ....New Zealand	Sukiyaki Sauce ....Japan
Rutabaga Pie ....Sweden	Summer Borscht ....Australia
Rye Rolls ....Sweden	Summer Soup ....Finland, Poland
St. Croix Sundae ....Virgin Islands	Sunshine Cake ....Bahama Islands
Salad Dish Marinade ....Poland	Swedish Coffee ....Sweden
Salsa du Carciofi ....Italy	Swedish Pancakes, Mushrooms..........Sweden
Sauce Vinaigrette ....Brazil	Swedish Rye Rolls ....Sweden
Sauteed Bananas ....Mexico	Sweet Basil Macaroni ....Italy
Sauteed Green Peppers ....Mexico	Sweet Farina Pudding ....Egypt
Savoury Rice...........................Hawaii	Swiss Chard ....Switzerland
Scalloped Apples (Brown Betty) ...G.B.-Scotland	Swiss Cheese Souffle ....Australia
Schillo (Indian Rice) ....India	Swiss Toast ....Morocco
Scottish Shortbread ..............G.B.-Scotland	Tapioca Pudding ....Australia
Scottish Shortbread ..............G.B.-Scotland	Tempura ....Japan
Scrambled Eggs (Chilaquiles) ....Mexico	Topaz Dressing ....Australia
Shish Koftesi (Kofta Fillings) ....Arabia	Tomato, Baked ....Arabia, Iran
Shortbread .......................G.B.-Scotland	Tomato, Broiled ....Egypt
Snow Peas, Mushrooms, Carrots ....China	Tomato Soup .....Australia, New Zealand, Spain
Soda Bread, Irish ....Ireland	Tomatoes, Stuffed ....Jamaica; Philippines
Soto Jam ....Indonesia	Tomatoes, Stewed ....Netherlands
Sour Cream Pimento Souffle ....Virgin Islands	Tossed Green Salad ....Brazil, U.S.
Southern Corn Bread .......................U.S.	Turkish Coffee ....Greece, Turkey
Spanakopita ....Greece	Turkish Delight ....Turkey
Spanish Custard, Flan ....Spain	Turnip Cups ....Poland
Speckled Bean Soup ....Hungary	Turnip Salad ....Russia
Spiced Coffee Viennese ....Austria	Ukrainian Egg Rissoles ....Russia
Spiced Tea ....Russia	Uncooked Applesauce..................Germany
Spicy Rangenak ....Iran	Vanilla Frosting ....Austria
Spinach, Creamed ....Australia, Ireland	Vanilla Poppy Seed Cake ....Austria
Spinach Salad ....Hawaii, U.S.	Vanilla Sugar ....Austria

Conversion Table

1 cup = 250 milliliters
¾ cup = 200 milliliters

5 milliliters = 1 teaspoon
15 milliliters = 1 tablespoon

4 liters = 1.06 gallons
1 liter = 1.06 quarts
500 milliliters = 1.06 pints

1 cup 250 milliliters
200 milliliters
¾ cup 150 milliliters
½ cup 100 milliliters
¼ cup 50 milliliters

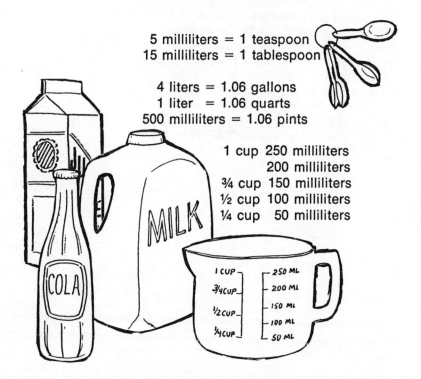